W0254656

INDIA CRIED THAT NIGHT

SUPRATIM SARKAR

INDIA CRIED THAT NIGHT

UNTOLD TALES OF FREEDOM'S FOOT SOLDIERS

Translated by Yajnaseni Chakraborty

RUPA

Published by
Rupa Publications India Pvt. Ltd 2018
7/16, Ansari Road, Daryaganj
New Delhi 110002

Sales Centres:
Allahabad Bengaluru Chennai
Hyderabad Jaipur Kathmandu
Kolkata Mumbai

Copyright © Supratim Sarkar 2018

Map and photographs courtesy Kolkata Police Archives

The incidents and facts in this book have been verified to the extent possible, and the author and publishers are not in any way liable for the same.

All rights reserved.
No part of this publication may be reproduced, transmitted, or stored in a retrieval system, in any form or by any means, electronic, mechanical, photocopying, recording or otherwise, without the prior permission of the publisher.

ISBN: 978-93-5304-370-4

First impression 2018

10 9 8 7 6 5 4 3 2 1

Printed and bound in India by Replika Press Pvt. Ltd.

The moral right of the author has been asserted.

This book is sold subject to the condition that it shall not, by way of trade or otherwise, be lent, resold, hired out, or otherwise circulated, without the publisher's prior consent, in any form of binding or cover other than that in which it is published.

CONTENTS

FOREWORD

Writing the foreword for the second book of a writer, whose first book *Murder in the City* was a runaway bestseller, can be a daunting task. The stories covered in *India Cried That Night* are not only of the extraordinary courage of young men and women, but also of our desire to determine our own fate as a nation. In this backdrop, writing a foreword for a book which is likely to find pride of place in the collection of many Indian book lovers can be a little unnerving. However, the flip side is that it gives one a chance to be part of a book which one expects is going to be another national bestseller and that thought is enough to squeeze a few lines out of the even most reticent.

This book covers ten true incidents to which Kolkata Police was first hand witness, all inspired by ideas of freedom and self-determination, except one special story which narrates an incident involving Nobel laureate Rabindranath Tagore.

It is difficult to check one's tears while reading about the sacrifices made by young boys and girls. Their driving force was the purity of purpose—neither money nor glory. Every tale is a reminder of the supreme sacrifices made to achieve freedom. What stands out in each tale is the selfless and pure devotion of the young men and women who unfortunately have not found any mention in our history books.

However, this book is not an effort to rewrite history but an attempt to underline the efforts and sacrifices of countless unsung heroes of the freedom movement of India. Kolkata Police has opened up its archives, so that the writer can, in his own inimitable style, narrate the true stories. This book does not present history as written by the winner or the vanquished but as written by a representative of a generation trying to grapple with the legacy of its forefathers and the role of Kolkata Police during that period.

Nelson Mandela's words, 'Real leaders must be ready to sacrifice all for the freedom of their people', capture the essence of the real leaders whose stories have been told in this book. We hope this book would be of value not only to the present generation but also the future ones.

Forty-two years ago (on 16 June 1976), the photograph of a dying 12-year-old Hector Pieterson being carried in the arms of a crying young man during the Soweto uprising in South Africa, shook the conscience of the world, and galvanized the struggle against apartheid. The image can be seen on Wikipedia at www.en.wikipedia.org/wiki/Hector_Pieterson#/media/File:Hector_pieterson.jpg. It will give you plenty of opportunity to ponder and reflect.

In terms of its impact, the shock and pain was similar to the horrific image of the screaming girl taken during the Vietnam War, as she ran naked down the road, her clothes and skin melted by a napalm bomb attack. That one photograph helped end a war. It also won the Pulitzer Prize.

The effort of publishing this book would be well worth it, if even one of its stories touches the reader's heart. I join all the ranks of Kolkata Police to salute these hitherto unsung heroes of our freedom struggle.

Rajeev Kumar
Commissioner of Police, Kolkata
16 June 2018

AUTHOR'S NOTE

Lalbazar. Known to everyone, particularly in West Bengal, as the headquarters of Kolkata Police. But this book is about a Lalbazar that few people know.

This is also a book about individuals who aroused the desire for freedom in a country oppressed for centuries. Again, a group of people who very few of us know.

It all began with a series of posts bearing the hashtag #days long gone on Kolkata Police's official Facebook page. The idea was to generate awareness about the lesser-known freedom fighters of Bengal, who nonetheless played a key role in the armed freedom movement, and how the authorities at Lalbazar tried all means, fair and foul, to thwart their nationalistic aspirations.

Most of the material for those posts came from a painstaking survey of the case files and documents preserved in the Kolkata Police's archives. The response from readers was highly encouraging, and the demand that the posts be published in book form grew steadily louder. So here it is.

The era commonly known as Agni Yug (Era of Fire) in Bengal, following the first partition of the province in 1905, was one of armed revolution. It has been extensively written about and researched, and there is absolutely no reason to assume that this book will in any way add to the corpus of scholarly and historical material that exists on the era. *India Cried That Night* looks back at the strategic and operational policies of Kolkata (Calcutta, then) Police, as they tried hard to combat a determined, fearless, focused group of young revolutionaries.

These are the revolutionaries whom time forgot. Their unimaginable valour and sacrifice never made it to the pages of mainstream history books. Researchers will know of Kanailal Bhattacharya or Birendranath Duttagupta. Historians will remember Habu Mitra or Sushil Sen. But what of the general populace?

The truth is inescapable. The majority of us have never ventured out of the circle created by the likes of Khudiram Bose, Prafulla Chaki, Master Da (Surya Sen), Bagha Jatin, Pritilata Waddedar, Matangini Hazra and Benoy–Badal–Dinesh. The unnamed heroes have never had their birth or death anniversaries observed, or their busts or photographs garlanded.

This is their book. It is an effort to repay the debts of one's predecessors. It is also an obligation to tell future generations of the immensely high price their nation paid for its freedom. Of the ten stories in this book, nine are about the running battle that Lalbazar fought against the revolutionaries. All the protagonists in these stories, with the possible exception of Benoy–Badal–Dinesh, are unknown to the ordinary reader.

That same reader is bound to notice that the sixth story has nothing to do with the freedom movement. Though it features one of its great stalwarts, Rabindranath Tagore. In all its years of operation, only once did Lalbazar come close to welcoming the Nobel laureate through its gates. That story cannot be kept out of a book on the unseen face of Lalbazar.

Readers are no strangers to historical and quasi-historical narratives based on the lives of popular national heroes. What they have seen less of are narratives in praise of unknown heroes. Those that do, exist as either dry documents or hagiographies.

This book is based on recorded facts subjected to a certain creative licence. The idea is to imbue readers with a sense of nostalgic tribute, rather than reinforce their aversion to dry history.

Of all those who wanted the Facebook posts to become a book, perhaps nobody was as passionate as Rajeev Kumar, commissioner of police, Kolkata. From the very beginning, all he said was, 'The coming generations really need to know how much the revolutionaries sacrificed. This book needs to be done.' His infectious enthusiasm and encouragement have provided a wealth of support to me. There is no end to the gratitude I feel for him because he is the reason this book has seen the light of day.

I'm also immensely grateful to Assistant Commissioner of Police (retd) Nihar Roy, who granted me access to a rich corpus of old books and documents from his personal collection. I am unable to quantify his contribution. To my junior colleague Indrajit Dutta, my thanks for not only helping me prepare the manuscript, but also cheerfully dealing with all the many demands I made of him.

Finally, in all works such as this, which depend heavily on history, there is always a chance of factual errors, despite all efforts. In such an eventuality, the responsibility rests solely with me.

Presenting *India Cried that Night*. A book in appearance, a tribute in spirit.

Kolkata
June 2018

Chapter 1

THE NOT-SO-GOOD BOY: SUSHIL SEN

'WELL, HE'S JUST a child!'

'Right Sir, still a minor, but he's full of fire. He didn't listen when he was asked to stop. Instead, he hit an officer!'

'What?!'

'Yes Sir, ran at him, shoved him and then punched him. The nerve! I'll put him in custody, shall I?'

'No...he's a juvenile...but he must pay for what he has done. Take him downstairs and give him fifteen strokes with the cane. No less than fifteen! Then let him go.'

'Right, Sir.'

The seething youth, his face showing no sign of remorse, his resistance obvious, is dragged downstairs from the second floor.

'This is totally...totally barbaric! Caning a child like that, again and again, in front of everyone...'

'He isn't human...the bloody animal.'

'This is beyond all limits! Our movement will lose its backbone if he can't be taught a lesson soon.'

'Agreed...but what the lesson will be...who will do the job, how...?'

'There can only be one lesson for the monster. Death. No right to live.'

'Agreed again…,but just wanting it means nothing. There are guards around all the time. It's difficult to even get close. Trying to kill him through all that security is suicide, pure and simple.'

'But we have to find a way! After this, how can we just sit idle?'

'What way?'

'A plan has been buzzing in my head…'

'What plan?'

This is a story set in the heart of Lalbazar. A story of times long forgotten and one that goes back over a century. India's independence is still a distant dream, and the Union Jack is still flying all over India.

In the first decade of the twentieth century, the freedom movement in Bengal is becoming more and more strident. The partition of Bengal in 1905 has ignited rage among the masses and inspired revolutionaries to launch an armed attack against administrative oppression. Secret revolutionary societies such as Anushilan Samiti and Jugantar are operating at full steam, forcing a desperate administration to issue blanket bans.

Simultaneously, patriotic writings in nationalistic publications such as *Bande Mataram* are having an uplifting influence on their readers, and so widespread is their appeal that the ruler's sceptre has been descending with equal ruthlessness on both writers and publishers. The same sceptre which, quite some time ago, had first appeared as a merchant's yardstick.

Part of what Lalbazar is today used to be the chief presidency magistrate's court in those days, witness to numerous sensational trials of Indian freedom fighters.

Magistrate D.H. Kingsford, who joined the Indian Civil Service (ICS) in 1894, is an alumnus of Trinity College, Cambridge. Having handled several important assignments in Bengal's districts, he is appointed chief presidency magistrate of Calcutta (now Kolkata) in 1906. Having mastered the Bengali language in no time, he moves into his first official residence at Hungerford Street, which later shifts to Kyd Street.

Kingsford expends most of his intellect, competence and efforts in tormenting freedom fighters, or even those in support of them. On 24 July 1907, he sentences Bhupendranath Dutta (younger brother of Swami Vivekananda) to a year's imprisonment, his crime being the publication of two anti-British essays in the newspaper *Jugantar*. While it goes without saying that a British judge cannot be sympathetic towards the aspirations for autonomy of a subjugated nation, that there's no question of the 'executioner feeling the pain of, and crying with, the executed' (to paraphrase Rabindranath Tagore), Kingsford seems to be setting new standards of cruelty by his actions.

A case is initiated against *Bande Mataram* too. The grounds are similar—outspoken opposition to an exploitative overlord. As the case progresses, several interested citizens, the majority of them spirited young men, crowd the court premises every day. The trial takes a dramatic turn when Bipin Chandra Pal refuses to testify against Aurobindo Ghosh, then editor of the publication.

Thousands of people now begin to throng the Lalbazar premises. Confronted with the problem of overflowing crowds shouting patriotic slogans, the British administration regularly instructs the police to resort to lathi charges, which are often brutal and indiscriminate.

On 26 August 1907, the tyrannical behaviour crosses the limits of endurance. The hearing is on, as usual, the crowd has gathered outside, and the cries of 'Bande Mataram' can be heard every now and then, also as usual. As the stream of people threatens to turn into a flood, the police, commanded by Inspector E.B. Huey, launch a lathi charge, as usual. What is not usual is that today, a gangly youth of about fifteen decides to give as good as he gets. His name is Sushil Sen, and he lands a few counter blows on the inspector. Inevitably, he loses the unequal fight, and is carted off to the magistrate's court.

Kingsford orders, 'Cane him fifteen times, with everyone watching, and let him go.' Such a punishment is in accordance with the Code of Criminal Procedure, 1898.

His instructions are obeyed. Historians have recorded the ensuing scene. With every slashing stroke of the cane, Sushil cries out, 'Bande Mataram!' Louder and louder. The sheer savagery of the beating induces an explosive anger in the helpless crowd, while Kingsford demonstrates a travesty of justice.

The outrage provokes intense reactions across Bengal. Kingsford now has a nickname—Kasai Qazi (Butcher Magistrate) among the revolutionaries. Even moderates such as Surendranath Banerjee are outspoken in their condemnation, while the hardliners decide that here is a sin unworthy of forgiveness. And so begins the operation to exterminate Kingsford.

'A plan has been buzzing in my head...'

'What plan?'

Born in Shillong in 1892, Sushil was the son of Kailash Chandra

Sen, head clerk at the Inspector General (IG) Prisons office. As he took his first steps into adolescence, the dominant national sentiment was one of resistance to the British. A gifted student, Sushil was awarded a double promotion in Shillong Government High School, and in 1905 he joined a secret society run by Gyanendranath Dhar in Sylhet to undergo special training in boxing and stick fighting. Inspired by Bipin Chandra Pal's speech at the Surma Valley Political Conference of 1906 in Sylhet, he travelled to Calcutta, and enrolled at National College while also training in gymnastics under Bipin Behari Ganguly.

Following the caning incident in August of 1907, Sushil finds himself elevated to the rank of a hero among the revolutionaries, and is even felicitated at College Square. The crowning glory of the event is the singing of a hugely popular song among revolutionaries of the time, written by Kaliprasanna Kabyabisharad:

> If (my) life ends, let it be done
> If they cane me, will I forget the 'mother'?
> Am I such a mother's son?

As Sushil's involvement in revolutionary activities grows steadily, the fearless teen is inducted into the 'slay Kingsford' plot. His task is to make several detailed recces of the magistrate's residence and its surroundings, which he does. What now?

Calcutta's administrative circles have been abuzz with speculation that Kingsford is to be transferred out of Calcutta. The revolutionaries are now desperate to execute their plan quickly. The planning has taken long enough, and the unanimous decision is that it will be unwise to delay the implementation any further.

As is usual when a government servant shifts to a new location, the act of wrapping up an entire household assumes precedence above all else. There is a deadline within which the new charge must be assumed, and failing the deadline inevitably draws the wrath of one's superior. The aim, therefore, is to somehow gather all of one's moveable belongings and rush to the destination, rather than neatly categorize every household article before carrying it off.

Kingsford is no exception. He has been transferred to Muzaffarpur, Bihar, and must take charge there as soon as possible. Chasing time, he sets off in a rush, his belongings packed into trucks.

The fact that radios, cycles, lunchboxes, wristwatches, laptops and innumerable other articles of daily use can be rigged to set off violent explosions is widely known in today's day and age. And courtesy the Internet, the technique of creating an improvised explosive device (IED) is easily accessible.

The story of one of the first IEDs in India, however, goes back more than a hundred years when technology was nowhere near as bountiful, nor was there a constant stream of information about the outside world. Nonetheless, because innovative thinking has never been a slave to technology, it was possible for the revolutionaries to devise their own IED, and come up with a 'book bomb'.

Kingsford's love of books is widely known, and in the days leading up to his departure, with a steady procession of farewell gifts making their way into his house, an aesthetically wrapped book can easily find its way in too. Kingsford will unwrap the book, open it and the resultant explosion will then do its job. That is the blueprint for the murder.

Hemchandra Das, a revolutionary from Midnapore, is handed the task of implementing the blueprint. In July of 1906, Hemchandra had travelled abroad to strengthen ties with various foreign revolutionary organizations and learn more about their workings. For example, in France, he learnt the intricacies of assembling a variety of explosives, and came back to India in 1907, accompanied by a Browning pistol and a manual on how to make bombs. Almost immediately upon his return, he joined Barin Ghosh's secret revolutionary society Jugantar and immersed himself in the freedom struggle. Small wonder, then, that he was entrusted with the job of converting a book into a bomb.

As Hemchandra gets down to it, the first question is, which book? It should be a book that will draw Kingsford's interest, forcing him to turn the pages. So which book? Finally, the conspirators conclude that as Kingsford is a judge and is in the habit of reading regularly for professional reasons, a law book ought to do the job.

They find a law book, *Commentaries on the Common Law: Designed as Introductory to Its Study* by Herbert Broom (1873), which has 1075 pages. Hemchandra leaves eighty pages from the beginning, and nearly four hundred pages from the end, untouched. The remaining six hundred-odd pages are neatly cut out to make a square space. The explosive ingredients—picric acid and fulminate of mercury—are stuffed into a cocoa tin, which is then placed in the carved-out hollow. Hemchandra then uses a spring to bind the book back together in such a manner that as soon as Kingsford opens it, the spring will instantly activate the ingredients, resulting in an explosion. The end of Kasai Qazi.

Posing as a government employee, Paresh Moulik, one of the revolutionaries, delivers the parcel to the guards posted at

Kingsford's residence. As the guards have seen many such farewell gifts since the announcement of Kingsford's transfer, the package is forwarded into the house without a trace of suspicion.

Destiny now steps in. Within the next two months, in a frantic rush to assume his new charge as district and sessions court judge in Muzaffarpur, Kingsford and his household leave Calcutta, the package still unopened. Trapped in a truck, the book bomb sets off for Muzaffarpur.

The rebels' run of bad luck doesn't end here. Immersed in work once he reaches his new posting, Kingsford relegates the critical parcel, along with several other farewell gifts, to a warehouse adjoining the stables in his bungalow, intending to go through them at leisure. The law book thus lies forgotten, and a few years are added to Kingsford's life.

Although distraught, the revolutionaries refuse to give up. In a few months, they put together a new plan, which is to dispatch two young men to Muzaffarpur with the task of killing Kingsford. Barin Ghosh selects the two assassins, Sushil Sen and Prafulla Chaki. In due course, the duo, disguised as Durgadas Sen and Dinesh Chandra Roy respectively, make an initial reconnaissance trip to Muzaffarpur, and twice inspect Kingsford's bungalow to make sure of its location, as well as to form an idea of their target's daily activities and routine.

Days before the all-important journey, however, Sushil's father falls critically ill, and is practically on his deathbed in their Sylhet home. His son stubbornly refuses to visit him until he has ended Kingsford's life. Using all their persuasive powers, Barin Ghosh,

Hemchandra and the others finally convince Sushil to go back to Sylhet to see his father one last time.

A substitute is found as Prafulla Chaki's companion. His name? Khudiram Bose.

The duo's subsequent daring yet doomed mission is by now so wellknown and so often discussed that details are superfluous here.

In the context of this narrative, the only relevant fact to emerge from the said mission is that as an immediate response to the failed attempt on Kingsford's life, police in Calcutta begin combing operations in search of rebel hideouts. Barin and Aurobindo are among the many arrested, and a huge cache of arms, explosives and ammunition is seized, leading to the famous trial in the Alipore Conspiracy Case. As part of their investigation into the case, the police finally learn of the book bomb still lying in Kingsford's warehouse from one of the arrested revolutionaries, and of the plot to kill Kasai Qazi. Nearly a year has passed since the bomb was sent to Kingsford, and it is now February 1908.

An extract from the Sedition Committee report of the British government reads, 'A well-known revolutionary, when in custody, said that a bomb had been sent to Mr Kingsford in a parcel. The parcel did not contain a book, but the middle portion of the leaves had been cut away and the volume was thus in effect a box and in the hollow was contained a bomb with a spring to cause the explosion if the book was opened.'

As they learn of the plot, the police instantly telegram Kingsford, and explosives expert Major Muspratt-Williams and his team set off for Muzaffarpur as though for a battle. The bomb is retrieved, brought back to Calcutta with the care it deserves, and defused in a garden adjoining the Kyd Street residence of Commissioner of Police Frederick Loch Halliday.

In his report dated 28 February 1908, Major Muspratt-Williams wrote:

> I proceeded to Muzaffarpore on the evening of the 22nd, arriving there next morning at 10 am and was met by Mr Kingsford, ICS and Mr Armstrong, Superintendent of Police.... I placed the bomb in my own hand bag, having first wrapped it in cotton wool, and I padded it all round with cotton wool taken out of a cushion. I then caught the afternoon train back to Calcutta on the morning of 24th ... I took the bomb to the compound of Mr F L Halliday, CIE, MVO, Commissioner of Police, and was accompanied by Mr Denhas, who kindly assisted me in conducting the operation, as also did Mr Halliday.

The major then went on to clearly state how fatally effective the explosive was. 'There is no doubt this would have been a most destructive bomb, had it exploded. That 'destructive bomb' has been carefully preserved at the Kolkata Police museum on Acharya Prafulla Chandra Road, as perhaps the earliest example of an IED devised in India.

To return to our narrative, in the years to follow, Sushil becomes even more active in the freedom movement. Always meritorious, he takes Aurobindo's advice and concentrates on further studies and finally graduates with a gold medal in Chemistry. As a student of Presidency College and an inmate of Eden Hindu Hostel, he meets Jatindranath Mukhopadhyay, or Bagha Jatin, who revives in him the desire to serve his country.

A hero's death claims Sushil in 1915 when he falls during a secret armed mission in Nadia, part of a team of six trapped in a deadly circle formed by British forces. Shot in both legs, Sushil is effectively immobilized, and the situation offers three options. One, complete surrender; two, continuing to fight till death; three, leaving Sushil behind and escaping to fight another day, a course of action that is out of the question for his comrades.

Sushil himself comes up with the fourth plan. Marshalling the beleaguered team, he is able to quickly and clearly explain to them the futility of dying together, a move that will ensure that their goal remains unattained forever. Instead, the death of one is preferable to collective suicide, so that those who survive can keep the fight alive. His comrades respect his final request. What remains of the twenty-three-year-old's life is extinguished, not by British bullets, but those of his own comrades.

So intense is his hatred for British oppression that Sushil refuses to surrender even in death. In a final, if gruesome, tribute, and once again following his orders, his companions chop up his body and bury the pieces in so scattered a manner that the British-Indian police have absolutely no chance of ever finding him.

'Sushil' (good/genteel in Bengali) was never a 'good' boy. Certainly not the kind of boy you could cane into forgetting his 'mother'.

Sushil Sen

Bipin Chandra Pal

Hemchandra Das

Kaliprasanna Kabyabisharad

D.H. Kingsford

Book bomb sent to D.H. Kingsford

D.H. Kingsford's bungalow, Muzaffarpur

Chapter 2

BATHED IN BLOOD: SATYEN BASU AND KANAILAL DUTTA

'NO, MA CAN never come here. I'm not seeing her. Ask her not to come.'

'She just wants to see you for a few minutes. Why are you doing this?'

'I said no…'

'Why not? Why can't she see you one last time? Why are you being so stubborn?'

'I'm not stubborn, I'm scared. I can't bear it if she breaks down. Try and understand.'

'Well, you should try and understand too.'

'All right then, you explain it to Ma. No crying, no tears. That'll make me weak.'

'She won't cry, we'll explain. Just say yes.'

'Yes…'

The discussion is low-voiced, almost whispered.

'What! He's going to talk? That will finish everything!'

'You think I don't know that? The traitor…'

'Are you sure he'll confess?'

'A hundred per cent. It was absolutely wrong to trust him. You're asking me if I'm sure—everyone knows. They've transferred him to a separate ward, to stop us from trying anything. There's extra security outside his cell.'

'So what? Let them guard him as much as they can. Death is a traitor's only punishment. How can he get away with framing all of us?'

'Death how? Who will kill him?'

'We'll need to decide. But we need a weapon first.'

'Won't be easy to bring arms in here, will it?'

'Nothing is easy, it depends on how you look at it. It's tough, yes, but we'll think of a way.'

'I just feel like throttling him right now...'

'Try something stupid like that, and you'll be stuffed with bullets in a few minutes. If you must die, take him with you.'

'Yes, kill him and die. All I need is a revolver...'

'Yes, we need arms, anyhow.'

The initial round of questioning is nearly done. One by one, the accused have been presented to Commissioner of Police Frederick Loch Halliday in his chamber. Now, one person remains. And he has been brought into the commissioner's chamber under armed guard. Even at a cursory glance, Commissioner Halliday realizes this man, in his mid-thirties, is different from the others. His wide eyes, serene face and unperturbed body language display a clear lack of anxiety. The commissioner's first question is blunt.

'Aren't you ashamed of being involved in this cowardly,

dastardly activity?'

The young man remains unmoved. 'What right have you to assume that I was involved?'

'I am not assuming, I know everything,' the commissioner snaps.

The response is calm, measured.

'What you know or do not know is your concern. I wholly deny having any connection with these murderous acts.'

The partition of Bengal in 1905 creates intense, angry ripples among the population. That anger proves to be the catalyst behind the birth of an aggressive form of nationalism, leading to the establishment of various secret revolutionary associations, and a surge in readership of such patriotic publications such as *Jugantar* and *Bande Mataram*.

Revolutionaries hand-pick a few representatives of a generally oppressive regime, and between the end of 1907 and April of 1908, make several attempts to assassinate them.

In December 1907, Bengal's Lieutenant Governor Sir Andrew Fraser escapes a bid on his life thanks to a failed attempt to blow up the tracks on which his train is travelling. The mayor of Chandernagore (now Chandannagar), L. Tardivel, particularly notorious for his oppressive tactics against the freedom fighters, also survives an attempted assassination.

The revolutionaries are third time unlucky when they try to kill the Chief Presidency Magistrate of Calcutta, Douglas Kingsford, by sending him a 'book bomb'. Wrapped as it is, the explosive travels with Kingsford to his new posting, Muzaffarpur, where he has been transferred in such a hurry that he hasn't had time to unwrap the parcel. Thanks to a tip-off from the Special Branch, the parcel is brought back to Calcutta from Muzaffarpur and the explosive defused.

The attempts to eliminate Kingsford continue, however. Two young men, Khudiram Bose and Prafulla Chaki, set off for Muzaffarpur, carrying explosives made by Ullaskar Dutta.

The rest of the story has been read and heard over and over. On the night of 30 April 1908, the two revolutionaries hurl a bomb at a horse carriage supposedly carrying Kingsford, but in reality containing two British women who are killed on the spot, while Kingsford, travelling behind the women in another carriage, enjoys a miraculous escape, again.

The deaths of two innocent White women cause a vehement reaction within the administration, and preparations begin instantly for a ferocious counter-attack.

Commissioner Halliday summons an emergency meeting at Lalbazar the very next day after the attack, and among those present are all the top officers of the Detective Department and the Special Branch. Following a prolonged discussion, a blueprint is drawn up for night-time raids and searches, and several groups are formed, each headed by a senior officer and a trusted informer. According to the plan, the police conduct combined raids across the city in search of possible rebel hideouts.

The Special Branch already knows that the villa at 32 Muraripukur Road in Maniktala is the cradle for various militant activities, and the information is largely accurate.

Aurobindo Ghosh's brother Barin is a firm believer in achieving independence through armed revolution, and to that ultimate end, he has launched a programme to train young potential rebels in various disciplines at the villa. Alongside sessions on yoga, the Gita and the Upanishads, there are regular classes on revolutionary movements in various parts of the world. There is the mandatory stick fighting–wrestling–jujutsu practice, while a large part of the curriculum is devoted to training in firearms and lessons on making explosives.

A search of the villa yields a massive haul of guns, bullets, other weapons, bombs and raw material for explosives. Night-time raids are also conducted at 28 Grey Street, 38/4 Nabakrishna Street, 15 Gopimohan Dutta Lane, 134 Harrison Road and 23 Scott Lane. Among the confiscated articles are an abundant stash of weapons, bombs and cartridges, and nationalist literature of various kinds.

Those arrested in the various raids include Aurobindo, Barin, Ullaskar, Hemchandra Das, Kanailal Dutta and several more. All of them spend the night in the Lalbazar lockup.

The next morning, Commissioner Halliday questions the captives, and tries to extract a confession out of Aurobindo.

'Aren't you ashamed of being involved in this cowardly, dastardly activity?'

'What right have you to assume that I was involved?'

Formally christened '*Emperor* vs *Barindra Ghosh and Others*', the trial becomes more popular as the Maniktala Bomb Case or the Alipore Conspiracy Case. Police operations against revolutionaries continue throughout the month of May. Narendranath Goswami (Naren henceforth), scion of a Srirampur zamindar family and an active member of Barin's secret outfit is taken into custody.

From the Midnapore residence of Satyendranath Basu, uncle to Aurobindo–Barin and nephew of Rajnarayan Basu, one of the leading lights of the Bengal Renaissance, an old gun and kukri are recovered, on the basis of which Satyendranath is not only charged under the Arms Act, but also implicated in the Alipore case. Close to forty revolutionaries are now lodged in Alipore Jail, later renamed Presidency Jail.

As the Alipore Conspiracy Case remains an eternal landmark in the history of India's Independence movement, it has been extensively written about and discussed, and recorded in its entirety in several publications. However, the details are not within the scope of this narrative. Here, the intention is simply to trace the course of history back to the trial during which, inside the confines of Alipore Jail, a few Bengali revolutionaries pulled off an act so sensational and audacious that it sent shock waves across the nation.

In the first phase of the trial, statements are being filed before the district magistrate of 24 Parganas. Almost immediately after Naren's statement is recorded, the news spreads around Alipore Jail like wildfire. In what has turned out to be a confessional statement, Naren names not only Aurobindo, but also Subodh Chandra Mullick, Charu Chandra Dutta and several others. In addition, he has agreed to turn approver for the Crown, to walk free in exchange. The authorities are now transferring him to the prison's European Ward, under the watch of a prison employee named Higgens, to keep him safe from the wrath of his fellow inmates.

Born as he was into luxury, Naren joined the revolutionary

cause more out of a desire to follow the current trend than a genuine wish to free his country, despite many examples of revolutionaries born into wealth making incredible sacrifices for the sake of the movement. Unsurprisingly, his desire to be a revolutionary proves short-lived in the face of prolonged persecution.

Naren is lodged in Ward 44, literally forty-four cells in a row, with natural restrictions on the entry of light and air. A lifetime of luxurious living compels him to quickly capitulate to the desire for material comforts, and release increasingly seems a more attractive option to revolution. So what if it comes at the cost of betrayal?

For the sake of context, it needs to be mentioned that during the time following Naren's confession, there is no clear agreement among the imprisoned revolutionaries about a future course of action. Forever a believer in extremism, and a strong opponent of non-violence, Barin is drawing up plans to sneak in guns, bullets and bombs into the prison and force an escape. On the contrary, the priority for Satyen–Kanailal–Hemchandra is extreme retribution for Naren's treachery. Without breathing a word of the plan to Barin, they merely seek his help in importing weapons into the prison. One critical conversation happens behind Barin's back.

'Yes, kill him and die. All I need is a revolver...'

'Yes, we need arms, anyhow.'

They find the arms. Sunday is designated as the visiting day for friends and families of prisoners, and in exchange for a nominal sum of money, Barin manages to make allies out of the guards responsible for screening the outsiders.

On 23 August, Sudhangshu Jiban Roy, a revolutionary from Chandernagore, arrives at the prison, ostensibly to visit Barin. As the guards look the other way, he passes a revolver to Barin through the bars of the cell. The following Sunday, Srish Ghosh, also from Chandernagore, passes a second revolver to Barin in exactly the same way. The latter hands over one to Kanai, and the other reaches Satyen, then under treatment at the prison hospital.

A few days earlier, Satyen had sent a message to Naren saying, 'I can't go on like this. I want to be an approver too.' Having received the message, Naren visits Satyen, telling him that the British government is prepared to release Satyen in exchange for his testimony.

On 1 September, Naren is scheduled to submit yet another confessional statement. Satyen and Kanai decide further delay is impossible. Once he has the revolver, Kanai feigns an agonizing stomach ache and gains admission to the hospital. On the night of 30 August, Satyen gets a prison employee, Anurup Das, to carry a message to Naren: 'Urgent. Kanai wants to turn approver, too. Absolutely must meet tomorrow morning'.

31 August 1908, Alipore Jail Hospital, 6.45 a.m.

As Naren arrives at the hospital, with the guard Higgens, Satyen and Kanai emerge in the second-floor ward corridor. The three chat for about a minute, with Higgens waiting a little distance away. Suddenly, the sound of gunfire catches him unawares. Getting over his shock, Higgens sees Satyen and Kanai, who have whisked revolvers out of their waistbands, shoot Naren at point-blank range.

The dispensary is not very far away, and a bleeding Naren starts to run towards it, screaming, 'Help! They're going to kill me!'

As Higgens gives chase, Kanai shoots again, catching the guard on the wrist. A few prisoners and hospital employees attempt to stage a token resistance, and Kanai now fires in the air. 'Move again and you're dead!'

Both Naren and Higgens are desperately trying to escape, rushing down the stairs towards the prison gates. Revolvers out in the open, Satyen and Kanai are in hot pursuit, in a scene eminently fit for the silver screen—two young men fiercely chasing two bleeding men through the premises of a prison.

As the bizarre group nears the gates, the jailor and a few of his colleagues, who are escorting a European prisoner named Linton to the hospital, catch sight of it. Kanai aims his revolver at them and shouts, 'Try to stop me and I'll shoot the lot of you!'

The jailor and his men are rooted to the spot, but Linton is not. In fact, he begins wrestling with Satyen, who shoots and misses. At the same instant, Linton hears a gunshot almost next to his ear, and looks around to see Naren lying face down in the gutter adjoining the prison pathway. Higgens has by now managed to put a safe distance between himself and his pursuers.

Linton, an enormous, solidly built man, possesses tremendous physical strength. He manages to snatch Satyen's revolver and fling it away. Kanai presses the trigger again, and this time, the target is Linton, who ducks his head swiftly to avoid the bullet, and then pounces on Kanai. In the ensuing tussle, Kanai's revolver too is tossed away. The prison employees finally overpower the disarmed rebels.

Naren is taken to the hospital, his body riddled with not one, not two, but nine bullets. Death is just a formality.

Naren's killing is not merely revenge for his treachery, however. It bears immense legal significance too. In the absence of the approver, the defence lawyer has no chance to question him, which makes his testimony meaningless, his statement of no account. Naren's death also means that his confession is now no longer admissible as evidence, which could have spelt danger for Aurobindo and his comrades during the trial.

In his account of the Alipore Jail murder on 31 August 1908 to the chief secretary, the commissioner of police has this to say:

> Government of Bengal, Political Department, Confidential
> File No. 160 (1–16) of 1908
> Confidential No. 1876-C. dated 31 August 1908
>
> To
> The Chief Secretary to the Government of Bengal,
> Calcutta
>
> Sir,
>
> I have the honour to report that this morning at about 7 a.m. an under-trial prisoner named Norendra Nath Goswami [*sic*], who had turned approver in the prosecution of some 34 persons now pending trial before the Sessions Judge of Alipore on charges under Sections 121, 121 A, I. P. C. etc., was shot by two co-undertrial prisoners named Kanai Lal Dutt [*sic*] and Satyendra Nath Bose [*sic*] in the Jail Hospital of the Alipore Central Jail.
>
> It appears that the prisoner Norendra Nath Goswami who had been intentionally kept separate from the other prisoners confined in the European Ward was brought, from that ward, to the Jail Hospital by a European Convict Overseer named

Higgens. Norendra Nath had apparently previously arranged to meet, at that time, in the Hospital, two fellow prisoners, who were already patients in the Jail Hospital, named Kanai Lal Dutt and Satyendra Nath Bose. He had apparently been approached by the second of these prisoners, who had pretended that he also wished to make a statement; and his visit was really in order to get this statement. Evidently it was however part of a plot to get Norendra Nath within striking distance for it appears that almost immediately on Norendra Nath's arrival on the landing, at the head of the staircase leading to the second story of the Hospital, these two prisoners opened fire on him with two revolvers which they had secreted on their persons. Higgens the Convict Overseer attempted to arrest one of them and was shot through the wrist.

Norendra Nath although shot in several places was not mortally hit and fled down the stairs, out of the Hospital Compound and along an alley way towards the gate.

The prisoner Kanai Lal Dutt pursued him and shot him fatally through the back. He was then secured by a Eurasian Prisoner named Linton.

The District Magistrate, Mr Marr immediately commenced a judicial enquiry in the case.

A Police investigation has been started but the accused have not as yet been questioned by the Police as to how they came into possession of the weapons.

The accused Kanai Lal Dutt is a native of Jantipara Serampore, Hooghly and Satyendra Nath Bose is a native of Midnapore where he was head of the 'National Volunteers'.

A telegram has been sent to the Director, Criminal

Intelligence, Simla, and a copy of this letter has also been sent to him.

A further report will be submitted.

I have the honour to be,

Sir,
Your most obedient servant,
F.L. Halliday
Commissioner of Police, Calcutta

The case of Naren's murder is disposed of with war-like efficiency. The jury find Kanai guilty, and the magistrate announces a sentence of death by hanging on 9 September. Since the verdict on Satyen is not unanimous due to lack of evidence, the case is referred to the high court, where he too is condemned to death.

As he reads out the sentence, the magistrate duly informs Kanai that he has a chance to appeal against the verdict in a higher court. Kanai's instant response is, 'Appeal? What appeal?'

The twenty-year-old is scheduled to be executed on 10 November 1908. As dawn breaks, Commissioner Halliday accompanied by senior officers from Lalbazar arrives at the prison. Kanai is taken to the hanging enclosure at 6.00 a.m., completely devoid of any anxiety. Eyewitness accounts state that right until the moment when the black cloth covered his face, before the noose was slipped around his neck, his slight smile did not falter.

One of the British police officers present at the hanging later asks Barin, 'How many more do you have like him?'

Barin remains silent, but smiles a little.

The course of the Alipore Conspiracy Case is followed with great eagerness by Bengali society, and there is a tidal wave of sympathy for the two young men charged with Naren's murder. The administration knows this too and the commissioner refuses to allow Kanai's funeral procession to travel along the thoroughfares. An order goes out that the cortège is to take the lanes and bylanes along Tolly Nulla to reach the crematorium. In apprehension of a law and order situation, three hundred jawans are summoned from the Reserve Force at Fort William.

The problem is, spontaneous emotions have rarely been controlled by force. When the procession, having traversed lanes that grow ever narrower, reaches the crematorium at Keoratala, the waiting crowd has reached unmanageable proportions. People ranging in age from eight to eighty are out on the street, waiting to greet the martyr, flower petals raining down from balconies lining the way.

There are women carrying garlands, ghee and sandal paste, and most of the elderly carry copies of the Bhagavad Gita. The roar of 'Bande Mataram' from countless young voices is turning into a cosmic sound wave. The flood of inconsolable mourners wanting to touch the martyr one last time has brought all traffic to a standstill.

As the soaring emotions are somehow brought under control and the young martyr's last rites performed, there is yet another eruption, as a frenzied crowd attempts to collect the ashes of a soul now one with the elements. The crematorium stands witness to a moment in which rage, discontent and grief unite in a rare trinity.

Satyen is to hang on 21 November. The hard lessons learnt at Kanai's funeral force the British administration to decide that this time, the last rites will be performed within the prison itself. And that is indeed what happened. His age at the time of death—twenty-six.

Days before the hanging, his mother asks to see him. Satyen flatly refuses.

'No, Ma can never come here. I'm not seeing her. Ask her not to come.'

'Why not?'

'I can't bear it if she breaks down... All right, she can come, but no crying.'

She keeps her promise. Meeting her son for the last time, she doesn't shed a single tear.

Without going into the progress of the trial and extending the course of this narrative, suffice it to say that the verdict was announced on 6 May 1909. Of the thirty-seven accused, Barin and Ullaskar were sentenced to death by hanging, which was later commuted by the high court to deportation for life. Four accused received ten years in prison, and three were sentenced to seven years. The rest were acquitted.

What of Aurobindo? A little way into the trial, barrister Chittaranjan Das took the stage as the principal counsel for the accused. Here is part of what he had to say in his emotionally charged closing arguments:

> My appeal to you, therefore, is that a man like this, who is being charged with the offences imputed to him, stands not only before the bar in this Court but stands before the bar of the High Court of History and my appeal to you is this: That

> long after this controversy is hushed in silence, long after this turmoil, this agitation ceases, long after he is dead and gone, he will be looked upon as a poet of patriotism, as a prophet of nationalism and a lover of humanity. Long after he is dead and gone, his words will be echoed and re-echoed not only in India, but across distant seas and lands. Therefore, I say that the man in his position is not only standing before the bar of this Court but before the bar of the High Court of History…

In the judge's chair was Charles Porten Beachcroft, who took the Indian Civil Service examination in the same year as Aurobindo, with the latter occupying a higher position on the merit list once the results were declared. Based on his scrutiny of all available evidence, Justice Beachcroft wrote:

> I now come to the case of Aurabinda [*sic*] Ghose, the most important accused in the case. He is the accused, whom more than any other the prosecution are anxious to have convicted and but for his presence in the dock there is no doubt that the case would have been finished long ago. It is partly for that reason that I have left his case till last of all and partly because the case against him depends to a very great extent, in fact almost entirely, upon association with other accused persons…
>
> The point is whether his writings & speeches, which in themselves seem to advocate nothing more than the regeneration of his country, taken with the facts proved against him in this case are sufficient to show that he was a member of the conspiracy. And taking all the evidence together I am of opinion that it falls short of such proof as would justify me in finding him guilty of so serious a charge.

Absolved of all charges, Aurobindo walked free, his unconditional release driven by two men, Kanailal Dutta and Satyen Basu, who went to their deaths within ten days of each other.

Their deaths were mere physical occurrences, but the history of the freedom struggle has ensured their immortality.

Kanailal Dutta

Satyen Basu

Kanailal Dutta (R) and Satyen Basu (L)
arrested after the murder of Narendranath Goswami

Charles Porten Beachcroft

F.L. Halliday

Bomb shells found at 134 Harrison Road

Aurobindo Ghosh

Barin Ghosh

Ullaskar Dutta

Chittaranjan Das

Narendranath Goswami

Chapter 3

THE 'BETRAYER': BIRENDRANATH DUTTAGUPTA

IT'S A SCENE straight out of a movie.

As he runs down the street, desperately brandishing a revolver, the police hard on his heels, the young man of eighteen or nineteen frequently looks back and shouts, 'Stop!'

Not that his warning has any effect. The police show no signs of stopping. The officer-in-charge realizes it's only a matter of time before the visibly exhausted young man is captured. How long will he run? And where will he run to?

It's January in Calcutta, and the hands of the clock are creeping up on 5.30 p.m. The rush hour crowd is rooted to the spot, watching the frantic spectacle unfold, as the police rapidly narrow the gap between themselves and the fugitive.

He can feel his breath running out, his brain no longer working as the police close in. What should he do now? Damn, two more men running at him from the opposite direction, men in uniform. Police again. Now what?

The words of the man he calls Dada (Bengali for elder brother) flash through his mind: 'Death is better than being captured by the English', Dada often says. He's right. A slow, tortuous death at the hands of the police is infinitely worse than a bullet to the head from his own loaded revolver. Game over.

What the hell is the boy talking about?

It takes a lot to reduce the long-time employee of Alipore Court to speechlessness. After all, he knows these young revolutionary types well. The police frequently haul them into the dock on various counts of sedition and treason. He has seen how fearless they are, but this! In just about an hour, the judge will deliver what is almost certain to be a death sentence, but not only is the boy completely indifferent, he's actually smiling as he makes his bizarre request.

'I'm really hungry right now, Sir. You know I'll be going back to that awful prison food. I'd really love some kochuri (stuffed puri) and shingara (Bengali version of the samosa). Go on, Sir, please get me some from the court canteen...'

The young man begins to laugh at the astounded expressions of the policemen and lawyers around him in the courtroom. And then repeats his request for the delicacies, from inside the court lockup. 'It's against the rules, I know, Sir. But I'm hardly asking for weapons. It's only kochuri and shingara... Go on, please Sir... Oh and yes, some rosogolla (an iconic Bengali dessert) would be perfect to finish things off...'

Rosogolla? Kochuri and shingara? For a murder accused in the courtroom? Has anyone heard of such a thing? For the police, the situation is unprecedented, and the officers go into a huddle. Finally, a phone call is made to Lalbazar, explaining the peculiar request. The response from Charles Tegart, lord and master of the Special Branch, is: 'Fair enough. He will be sent to the gallows anyway in about a month's time. Give him whatever he wants. Keep him happy, we need him for something else too.'

And so, as the court breaks for lunch, a plateful of kochuri–shingara–rosogolla is placed before the accused. The boy happily polishes it all off, and is back in the box after his meal, waiting to go through the formalities. For this trial *is* a mere formality, everyone knows what the judge is about to say.

'You call this man your guru? This man?'

Mockery dripping from every word, the police officer holds up a page from a newspaper for the young man to see.

'Come on, take a good look...look at what he really is...and he is your guru...you call him Dada. One word from him, and boys like you are happily ready to die!'

In his prison cell, the youth sits wordless, his gaze fixed on the page and the photograph. The officer's words pierce his ears like arrows.

'Look at the photo...read the report...what? Can't believe your eyes?'

The nineteen-year-old really does wish he could disbelieve his eyes. What he's looking at can't be true, it isn't possible. Dada couldn't have done such a thing. But what about the report? The printed word? It clearly says Dada has been helping the police gather evidence against him, and has even made a statement. The accompanying photograph shows the familiar, self-assured figure. His thoughts are interrupted by the officer's scornful remarks, again.

'I've told you before, this Dada is ruining your lives. And you people, without thinking things through, are getting ready to hang like idiots. Do you know how close your Dada secretly is to the bosses in Lalbazar? Wait and see, he'll get off without a scratch. At most, a year or two in prison. And you? You'll be dead in a few days. Think about it...your death sentence won't change. But how can you watch him go free again and again, while you and your friends suffer?'

By now, the young man has sunk his face into his hands. The officer goes on remorselessly.

'Since the day we caught you, we've known whose plan you were following when you killed. But you've been telling us the same thing all through, "Whatever I've done, I've done on my own." Tell us the truth, there's still time. If you suffer, so should he. Now you know what he's really like, at least tell us now!'

Finally, the young man raises his head, his face a map of anger, despair and hurt. The officer isn't wrong, really. He has been blindly following Dada's orders, ready to sacrifice his life, and Dada has sided with the police? What's the point of the cover-up, then? He makes up his wounded mind.

'I'll tell you, Sir. I did it because Dada asked me to. He said...'

Hiding his excitement as best he can, the officer emerges from the cell. A message immediately goes out to Lalbazar: 'Mission accomplished. We have a confession. It is as we thought...the boy did the job, but the strings were pulled by their Dada...Bagha Jatin. The boy gave in once he saw the report and the photo.'

Tegart does not waste a second. He can't afford to. Gathering his men, he leaves Lalbazar for the prison cell in Alipore Jail, where a young man, condemned to hang by the neck until dead, hasn't been able to stop weeping.

You're the apple of their eyes
And the curse of ours
Oh, when will your home be wrecked
And you'll see stars!

That little rhyme was very popular among revolutionaries in Bengal in those days. The object of their derision: the infamous CID Deputy Superintendent of Police (DSP), Shamsul Alam.

The year is 1910. A few months have elapsed since the judicial sentence on the sensational Alipore Conspiracy Case was delivered on 6 May 1909. Principal accused Aurobindo Ghosh has been set free, while Barin Ghosh and Ullaskar Dutta are to hang. Hemchandra Das and ten others are set to be deported. Four accused have received ten years in prison, three more have got seven years. All the accused have appealed against the verdicts in the high court, and the hearing is currently on.

DSP Alam is the right-hand man of Eardley Norton, counsel for the prosecution in the case. A veteran of the force, DSP Alam is held in high esteem within the British establishment and has earned the respect of no less a man than Tegart.

There are several reasons for his place in the government's good books. Nobody lays out evidence against those accused of treason quite the way he does because he does a clean job of doing dirty things, as adept at gathering false testimonies as he is in brainwashing youngsters into turning approvers and witnesses for the Crown.

The Alipore Conspiracy Case has turned into a matter of prestige for the British administration. And Lalbazar is sparing no efforts to ensure that those arrested are adequately punished.

Work on gathering foolproof evidence for the high court hearing is gaining momentum. And the driving force is DSP

Alam, who has realized that should he manage victory for the government in this case, he will scale several steps on his way to the peak of his career. So he lives and breathes the case, endlessly scanning files, documents, statements and legal books, and spends hours in discussion with prosecutor Norton at the high court.

As can be expected for such an officer, his name has made it to the rebels' hit list. They know the case will slow down to a limp if he is removed; not many officers can match his thoroughness when it comes to preparing case documents. So the scheme to make the 'apple of their eyes' and the 'curse of ours' 'see stars' gets underway.

At this time, all the numerous rebel groups in Bengal making life difficult for the British administration, with their fearless and militant activism, unofficially acknowledge one man as their supreme commander—Jatindranath Mukhopadhyay—Jatin to his seniors, Dada to his junior comrades. A man who has earned the epithet 'Bagha' Jatin for fighting and killing a tiger, or 'bagh', armed with nothing but a kukri. A man whose charisma inspires his Young Turk followers to gamble on their lives without a second thought. And the man who the police are aggressively determined to put behind bars for a long time, by hook or by crook. The strategy is clear: if you can finish off the general, well and good; if not, at least imprison him for a long time, and his demoralized troops will scatter of their own accord.

Jatindranath awards the task of killing DSP Alam to a young man he is particularly fond of, called Biren or Birendranath Duttagupta of Bikrampur, Dhaka. Blessed with a physique that seems hewn in stone, and sparkling eyes that instantly draw attention, Biren has been intimately associated with rebel groups since his adolescence, committed to the sacred mission of freeing his country. He has been introduced to Bagha Jatin through

Gyanendranath Mitra of Beadon Street, whom Bagha Jatin trusts unreservedly.

The nearly nineteen-year-old Biren is a man of indomitable courage and single-minded passion. His joy at being chosen to kill DSP Alam is almost limitless. Of the hundreds of boys who surround Dada at all times, it is he who has been given the honour to kill that monster of an officer. He can hardly believe his luck.

As soon as the potential assassin has been identified, preparations begin for the actual killing. Such a decision, once taken, needs to be backed by a flawless blueprint. DSP Alam isn't merely a powerful official, but a highly intelligent man who knows all about the sarcastic rhymes in his honour, as well as the threat to his life. Vigilant in his movements, he is always accompanied by an armed guard, and he himself carries a firearm at all times. Above all, he is careful not to use the same route to work from home as he does from work to home. No aspect of his life is routine, personal or professional.

Nonetheless, Biren has to know DSP Alam's movements well, and the man to guide him is Satish Chandra Sarkar, a close associate of Bagha Jatin's. Satish points out all the possible locations to Biren, including not just the DSP's home and office, but both the Alipore and high court premises, where DSP Alam is spending so much time with Norton these days.

Location scouting done, what about the murder weapon? Bagha Jatin does the honours, courtesy Suresh Chandra Majumdar (nickname Poran, later to become the founder of *Anandabazar Patrika*), who hands Bagha Jatin a six-chamber revolver. Suresh had stolen the revolver himself, nearly five years ago in December of 1905, from the custody of Deputy Magistrate Raibahadur P.C. Moulik, who he knew. Suresh had met Bagha Jatin through an uncle of the latter's, Lalit Chatterjee, a lawyer and out-and-out nationalist. As an aside, Lalit was also related to iconic Bengali actor Soumitra Chattopadhyay.

In 1911, senior Criminal Investigation Department (CID) official F.C. Daly was to write in his report, 'The weapon with which the murder was committed belonged to a Deputy Magistrate of Cuttack District, who had lost it when he visited Calcutta and which was stolen by a youth named Suresh Mazumdar alias Poran. Poran later made it over to Jatin Mukherjee who had employed Biren Dutta Gupta to commit the deed.'

The first attempt is made in Chowringhee, at the beginning of the third week of January. DSP Alam leaves the high court to supervise another case, and Biren follows. However, he hasn't accounted for the large police presence around the DSP. Forget shooting at him, he can't even get close enough. The attempt ends in failure.

However, there's no question of failure on 24 January 1910.

Arriving at the high court a little late in the afternoon, and having sat in Norton's chamber as usual, laden with important documents related to the case, DSP Alam is ready to depart around 5.00 p.m., and alerts his guard.

'I'm about to leave. Is the car ready?'

The car is ready, so is Biren. He has met Satish Chandra Sarkar at Cornwallis Square that afternoon, and a loaded revolver and knife have changed hands. Satish has also escorted Biren to the court.

Having carefully observed DSP Alam's movements for about a fortnight, Biren has decided that if he has to kill him, he needs to do it when the DSP leaves the court. Granted, there are plenty of policemen around, and the risks are high, but there's no alternative. DSP Alam is in a car whenever he travels, and the police presence around the CID office is even larger. No, it has to be when he leaves the court.

As DSP Alam leaves the prosecutor's chamber, the advocate general, who was also part of the discussion, walks ahead of him. His armed guard is behind him. About to take the first step on the eastern staircase, DSP Alam is confronted by his messenger of death.

Faced with the grim young stranger, DSP Alam is taken aback for a moment, by which time his guard has noticed that the youth is extracting a revolver from inside his vest. Before the guard can prevent him, 'boom!' Biren has taken the shot from a handshaking distance, and the bullet pierces DSP Alam's chest. As he lies dying, the DSP utters the single word, 'Pakdo (Get him)!'

The police have every intention of getting him. The court premises are in an uproar, and the crowd around the DSP's body is as large as the one outside the court. 'Murder! Murder!' The horrified cry goes down the road, where Biren has descended with great swiftness, and has begun to run.

But he has nowhere to run in the dense crowd. A mounted policeman who gives chase is caught in the throng, too. Assuming a grievous crime has been committed, a few bystanders join the chase, forcing Biren to fire a warning shot in the air. The civilians fall back, the police do not. An officer on duty inside the court continues the chase with his men. The news reaches Lalbazar, 'DSP Shamsul Alam shot dead in High Court by unknown youth.' An armed unit of the Reserve Force scrambles to cover the short distance between the high court and Lalbazar.

By the time Biren has run down Old Post Office Street adjacent to the high court and reached Hastings Street (Kiran Shankar Roy

Road today), he is out of breath, his brain refusing to cooperate. Not only is the gap between him and his pursuers narrowing rapidly, he can see a few policemen running at him from the opposite direction. What now?

For a moment, Biren is overcome by the situation. By the time he gets over his hesitation and settles on suicide, a sergeant is almost face to face with him, and before Biren can hold the revolver to his own head, the sergeant has grabbed his hand. The policemen giving chase have also reached him, and Biren's chance to end it all on his own terms has vanished. Forced to surrender, he has to watch as his revolver, cartridges and knife are confiscated.

Then begins a period of relentless agony, as Biren is tortured for information about the conspiracy behind the assassination. Hardened officers of the CID and Special Branch spend hours grilling him, in vain. Biren does not say a word other than, 'I was angry with the DSP for the way he arrested and tortured revolutionaries. Whatever I have done, I have done on my own. I followed no instructions. I wanted vengeance, and got it.'

Over and over, like a broken record.

The accused has admitted his guilt, and let it be known that he has nothing to say in his defence. Justice is delivered swiftly. The verdict is death, and the hanging will take place on 21 February 1910. As the judge prepares to leave for lunch, with the sentence to be delivered in the afternoon session, comes Biren's smiling, bizarre request: 'I really feel like some kochuri and shingara today, Sir...please get me some from the canteen...'

And the orders from Lalbazar: 'Give him whatever he wants. Keep him happy, we need him for something else, too.'

'Something else' is the plan to imprison Bagha Jatin, and to find a way to get him to the gallows by implicating him in the murder conspiracy. In the days leading up to DSP Alam's killing, Howrah has witnessed a series of daring robberies. Accused of being involved in them, Bagha Jatin is arrested from 275 Upper Chitpur Road on 27 January 1910. Lalit is arrested on the same charge from Krishnanagar and Suresh Majumdar from Calcutta. A case is started under Section 400 of the Indian Penal Code, which becomes known as the Howrah Gang Case, and the accused are lodged in Howrah Jail.

Tegart now resorts to a cruel trick in his efforts to prove Bagha Jatin's involvement in the DSP's assassination. Faced with Biren's steadfast refusal to talk, he has a page of a newspaper printed, and so perfect is the fake that there is no question of it being challenged. That page carries a detailed report of how Bagha Jatin has helped gather evidence against Biren, alongside Bagha Jatin's photograph. That is the page the police show Biren on the morning of 19 February and the emotional manipulation begins.

'Do you know how close your Dada secretly is to the bosses in Lalbazar? Wait and see, he'll get off without a scratch. At most, a year or two in prison. And you? You'll be dead in a few days. You call this man your guru?'

Unable to withstand the mind games beyond a point, Biren breaks down. 'I'll tell you, Sir. I did it because Dada asked me to. He said...'

Tegart and his officers rush to Alipore Jail. There's no time, Biren is to be hanged the day after the next. His statement is recorded on a war footing, and Bagha Jatin's name enters the Shamsul murder case. Bagha Jatin is hurriedly transferred from

Howrah to Alipore, where a chief presidency magistrate's court is set up overnight, thanks to a special request from the police.

But Bagha Jatin's counsel now makes a countermove, stating clearly that he will be unable to cross-examine Biren, since he hasn't been given the time for even a basic discussion with his own client.

The police bosses now rush to the lieutenant governor, with an application to delay Biren's hanging by a week, so that Bagha Jatin's counsel cannot cite lack of time as an excuse. The application is rejected, the date remains 21 February.

The government didn't stop trying, though, not even after the hanging. The argument submitted to the court was that since the magistrate himself had recorded Biren's statement, it ought to be admissible in a case of murder, regardless of whether or not Bagha Jatin's counsel interrogated Biren. That argument was rejected by the high court.

Biren spent the day before his hanging in utter misery. Never in his worst nightmares had he imagined testifying against Dada. Had there been a mistake somewhere?

That same night, Biren learnt that there had, indeed, been a 'mistake', thanks to a prison officer, who couldn't come to terms with the idea that Biren would go to his death not knowing the truth. Devastated as he learnt of the fake newspaper trick, Biren pleaded with the officer to carry a message begging forgiveness, to Bagha Jatin.

That message reached Bagha Jatin only after the hanging, not that it was necessary. He knew for a fact that Biren would never have named him unless severely misdirected.

It has been nearly 108 years since Biren Duttagupta left us forever. Experts and researchers conversant with that era will know his name, but what about ordinary people like you and me? Have we heard of him, kept an account of his sacrifice?

Easy question, easy answer…

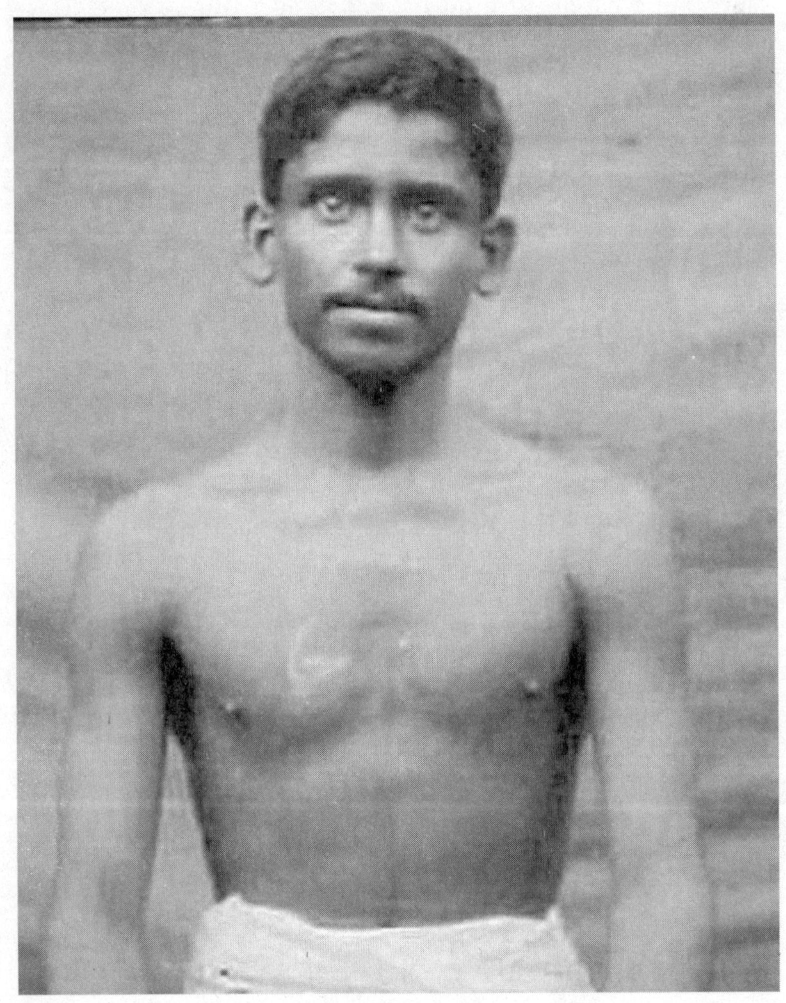

Birendranath Duttagupta

Bagha Jatin

Suresh Chandra Majumdar

Charles Tegart

Chapter 4

THE GREATEST DAYLIGHT ROBBERY: HABU MITRA

'WE'RE RUNNING OUT of bullets…'

'Right… How much longer?'

'At best, fifteen minutes…we're surrounded, no way out.'

The young man, clearly the undisputed leader on this battlefield of hits and counterhits, erupts in response. 'What do you mean, way out? Are we thinking of escape? What we need is a tactical retreat.'

'That's what I meant. Don't see any chance of that either.'

'We'll just have to fight to the end, there's no other way.'

'Yes… Watch out! Platoon coming up to the right!'

'Seen it! Fire!'

And so the silence of the riverside forest surrenders to the reverberating sounds of gunfire.

In a narrow room of Marwari Hostel in the west of Marcus Square, near College Street, a make-up session is in progress. A young man sits on a chair, while another stands behind him. For nearly the whole of the past hour, the latter has been running a pair of scissors through the seated youth's hair, with intense concentration. Clearly tired of sitting still at a stretch, the first young man is growing restless.

'How much shorter are you cutting it? My hair's beginning to look like an upturned bowl.'

'Be quiet and sit still. Biharis have even shorter hair.'

'Right, just shave it all off while you're at it.'

'I'd do it too, if need be. But this is enough for now.'

'Thank heavens, can I get up?'

'Yes. Don't forget the khaini (chewing tobacco) in the drawer.'

'Can't I chew paan instead?'

'No. Khaini. You don't have to chew it, just keep the box with you and pretend to have some. And that streak of choon (lime) on your palm needs to stay.'

'Got it. Anything else?'

'One more thing. Wear this dhukdhuki (good luck charm) around your neck.'

'What on earth is this?'

'Told you... dhukdhuki... made of brass... very common in Bihar.'

Once everything is in place, the young man finally stands in front of the mirror, and is taken completely aback. Looking at him, no one would see a true-blue Bengali. He's Bihari, right down to the smallest detail.

The well-built young man is visibly agitated as he castigates his comrades for their flights of fancy, as he calls them.

'Are you all mad? This can't happen... simply impossible.'

'No need to be so agitated. Why can't it? What's impossible?'

'Just because this meeting is being held near Lalbazar, you assume the operation will be possible right under their noses too? That simple, is it?'

'Nothing is impossible if the planning is right.'

'Have you thought what may happen if you put even a toe out of line? Police headquarters within a hundred metres, and the patrolling has increased of late. Plainclothesmen are everywhere now. There's some other way, you must think.'

'That may be, but where's the time? We need to be quick... such chances don't come often. We have to risk it.'

'I disagree. Do what you must, but I won't be part of it. Hope you pull this off.'

The tall young man walks out of the secret meeting being held at Chhatawala Gali, a stone's throw from Lalbazar. Night claims the evening as the clock inches toward 9.00 p.m.

The others sit down with a map. They need to know the geography of the area by heart, and a few red marks begin to appear around important landmarks—Dalhousie Square, Lalbazar, Customs House, British India Street, Malanga Lane, Hind Cinema...

His face a picture of suppressed fury, Special Branch Chief Charles Tegart holds up a copy of *The Statesman*, in which a front-page headline reads: 'The Greatest Daylight Robbery'.

Soon enough, Tegart's wrath rains down on his colleagues.

'So gentlemen, how has all this happened right under our noses? You think there is anything more embarrassing than this?'

An emergency meeting has been summoned at the Special Branch office on Elysium Row (Lord Sinha Road today). The officers listen to Tegart, heads bowed. So complete is the silence that the dropping of a pin will, no doubt, seem like an explosion.

'Officers, I want recovery at any cost and within the quickest possible time. Do whatever it takes. I won't take any excuses this time. They just can't get away with this.'

The men listen well, and realize that the all-powerful Tegart has been hit where it hurts: his pride in his professional competence. This is one case in which he will not tolerate the slightest laxity. Particularly since his razor-sharp mind and professional capabilities have raised him to the status of a legend within the British administration.

Global politics is becoming increasingly turbulent by mid-1914, as bilateral equations between countries undergo radical changes, and polarization prepares the ground for open combat. On 28 July, Austria–Hungary declares war on Serbia in retaliation for the assassination of Austrian Archduke Franz Ferdinand.

In the countdown to World War I, allies of the warring nations are gradually sucked into the vortex. Germany leads the Axis Powers of Austria–Hungary–Bulgaria versus the Allied Powers of Serbia–Russia–France–Japan–United Kingdom. The war begins, and lasts more than four years, with Italy–Romania–United States eventually joining the Allied Powers.

It is against this tumultuous backdrop of war that Rashbehari Bose, Jatindranath Mukhopadhyay (Bagha Jatin) and other

Bengali revolutionaries begin planning an armed uprising. The majority of the rebels are of the opinion that the time is right to further plague the British Raj with a constant series of attacks.

The British administration is not entirely unaware of these designs. The government machinery is active in trying to prevent the secret societies from further harassing the rulers, taking advantage of the war. Search operations are relentless, as what the revolutionaries need most at the moment are modern firearms, without which the dream of an armed uprising can never become reality.

Situated in the north-east corner of Wellington Square, and founded in 1897, the Atmonnati Samiti (roughly, Self-improvement Association) was led by Bipin Behari Ganguly, Anukul Chandra Mukherjee and others. In early August of 1914, Anukul learns of the impending arrival of the ship *Tactician* on 26 August, bearing a large quantity of government-requisitioned, state-of-the-art arms and ammunition to Calcutta, to be stored in a Vansittart Row warehouse behind the offices of leading arms importing company R.B. Rodda at 2 Wellesley Place. Included in the consignment are Mauser pistols and their ammunition.

Its unique operating system has made the Mauser pistol a particular favourite among the revolutionaries. With an effective range of five hundred yards, it is obviously a pistol, but if its containing wooden shell is attached to it, it can just as well be used as a longer range weapon, positioned on the shooter's shoulder, like a rifle.

Since this is an opportunity the rebels do not want to miss, the decision is made to hijack the consignment, with the blessings of Bipin Behari Ganguly and Bagha Jatin. So on 24 August, a secret meeting of revolutionaries is held at Chhatawala Gali, close to Lalbazar. Srish Pal and Haridas Dutta, two representatives of Hemchandra Ghosh's Mukti Sangha in Dhaka, are in Calcutta, and Srish is entrusted with the task of planning the operation.

As he is explaining exactly how the hijack attempt will be staged, Srish faces opposition from Narendranath Bhattacharya (to become famous as M.N. Roy in later years) who bluntly labels the operation as a flight of fancy.

'I disagree. Do what you must, but I won't be part of it. Hope you pull this off.'

Narendranath leaves. The rest sit down with a map. Srish begins pointing out geographical landmarks.

'Look at the map carefully, all of you. This is Lalbazar...and here's British India Street...'

26 August 1914, 11.00 a.m. The office area of Dalhousie is abuzz with the familiar hustle of a regular working day, as is the routine. The unending stream of traffic disgorges several commuters, and then takes in several more. The very air smells of activity.

Armed with all the necessary documents, Srish Chandra 'Habu' Mitra, a trusted employee of R.B. Rodda, waits in front of Customs House, very close to where the Reserve Bank of India building stands on Netaji Subhas Road today. Anglicized in bearing and attire, Habu is in trousers, immaculate half-sleeved shirt and polished boots. An impressive moustache complements his well-built frame, and on first sight, he justifiably evokes respect.

Seven bullock carts wait to transport the consignment. The

driver of the seventh cart, having arrived about five minutes behind the rest, has already been the target of Habu's ire.

'Stupid fool, why couldn't you hurry?' Habu bellows at the sheepish, downcast man.

A total of 202 wooden cases bearing the consignment are finally released. Of these, 192 are loaded into six carts, while 10 go into the tardy seventh cart. All the cases bear the initials of the company, RBR.

At most 100 or 150 metres from Lalbazar, the carts set off in a row from Customs House, bound for the Vansittart Row warehouse. Habu walks between the fifth and sixth carts, as the supervisor. As the first six carts veer off to the right from the thoroughfare, the seventh makes its way eastwards, unnoticed. Past Mango Lane, British India Street, Bentinck Street and Chandni Chowk, it sets a course for Malanga Lane, near Wellington. Mission Row, or Ganesh Chandra Avenue, had not come into being as yet.

Twisting the bullock's tail to make it go faster, the driver of the cart, with his close-cropped hair and a box of khaini in his pocket, his palm smeared with choon and a dhukdhuki around his neck, chuckles to himself as he thinks of the previous night and his flawless disguise.

'How much shorter are you cutting it? My hair's beginning to look like an upturned bowl.'

'Be quiet and sit still. Biharis have even shorter hair.'

At the warehouse, Habu is at his wits' end. Where in the name of heaven is the seventh cart? It was carrying the most valuable burden, according to the list that he had checked before leaving Customs House. There were ten cases, eight numbered from 396 to 403, each bearing 5,000 Mauser bullets. Case number 404 had 6,000 bullets. The remaining case, numbered 828, contained fifty .303 bore Mauser pistols. A total of 46,000 bullets and 50 Mausers, gone? This is a disaster…

Habu leaves immediately in search of the missing cart…and never returns. Actually, he isn't supposed to.

Because he's the star performer in this little heist!

Born in Raspur village of Howrah in 1890, Habu spent his childhood in his maternal uncle's home at 14 Das Lane in Calcutta's Malanga area. Never very academically inclined, he was known more for his daredevilry around the neighbourhood.

Anukul of the Atmonnati Samiti was a resident of 39 Malanga Lane. Always on the lookout for youths whom he could inspire to join the freedom movement, he noticed the daredevil Habu soon enough, and took him along to the association's gymnasium. Two years of training in boxing, stick fighting and physical drills ensued. At the end of it, with Habu now a strong, robust young man, Anukul helped him find a storekeeper's job with J.F. Madan Co.

In August of 1913, Habu finds a position at R.B. Rodda, thanks to a friend of Bipin Behari Ganguly, on a monthly salary of Rs 30. Very soon, his hard work and competence draw the attention of the owner, Mr Prike, and Habu is quickly elevated to the post of jetty clerk, entrusted with the job of getting imported consignments released. By August 1914, Habu has smoothly got consignments cleared forty times, and his employer sees in him a man to rely on.

It is Habu who tips off Anukul about the ship's load of Mauser pistols and bullets. The revolutionaries then draw up a faultless plan for the heist. Habu is among those present at the Chhatawala Gali secret meeting. As that meeting ends, another one begins in Habu's house, a little later that night, where it is decided that Anukul will arrange for a bullock cart, to be driven by Haridas, disguised as a Bihari. At a short distance from the cart, on both its flanks, Srish and Khagen Das will walk along, revolvers tucked into their waists. Four others—Suresh Chakraborty, Biman Ghosh, Ashutosh Roy and Jagat Ghosh—are charged with watching out for plainclothes policemen around Dalhousie Square, and singing loudly, should they notice anything untoward, to alert Haridas and his companions.

On the eve of the heist, Prabhu Dayal Himatsingka, originally of Dumka in Bihar, is the man who takes great pains to get Haridas into his disguise. An out-and-out patriot, Prabhu Dayal was also a dedicated social activist, and later became a renowned solicitor.

So smooth and clever is the heist that, until Prike lodges a complaint with Waterloo Street police station (Hare Street police station was yet to be established) three days later, Lalbazar has not the faintest idea that it has occurred. Prike knows the company will face administrative action on grounds of negligence, and so when three days of hunting prove fruitless, he has no choice but to go to the police.

Police Commissioner Frederick Loch Halliday and the Lalbazar top brass are thunderstruck. Such a large quantity of arms and ammunition in the hands of revolutionaries, in these war-torn times, snatched from right under Lalbazar's nose? The police go on the chase with all they have, and Tegart's anger gives the detectives sleepless nights.

'Officers… I want recovery at any cost and within the quickest possible time. Do whatever it takes. I won't take any excuses this time. They just can't get away with this.'

On 27 September, Haridas is arrested from 34 Shibthakur Lane, and a trunk full of bullets is confiscated. His memoirs record the moments following his arrest and transportation to the police station. Tegart and other senior officials arrive as soon as they learn of his arrest, and Tegart beams at Haridas, 'Hello Royal Bengal Tiger! Now you are bagged!'

Tegart's exultation is short-lived, however. Once the bullets are counted, the confiscated trunk is found to contain a total of 21,200 rounds. The next day, a hideout at 61/1/1 Kanulal Lane yields another 1,040 rounds. Searches and seizures through the remaining months of the year help recover another 960 rounds and two pistols. That's 23,200 rounds. What about the other bullets? And pistols?

This is what the police's annual report has to say about the entire incident:

> Annual Report on the Police Administration of the Town of Calcutta and its Suburbs, 1914 [page 12]
>
> On the 26th August 50 Mauser pistols and 46,000 rounds of ammunition were stolen by Srish Chunder Mittra [*sic*], the Customs House sirkar of Messrs. R B Rodda & Co. This sirkar

> was entrusted by the firm with the necessary documents and papers for clearing a consignment of arms and ammunition from the Customs House and took delivery of the goods. One cart containing the abovementioned Mauser pistols and ammunition was diverted from a string of seven carts on the way from Customs House and was eventually traced to an iron yard off Wellington Street where it was found that the arms [and] ammunition had been removed from the carts and stolen. Srish Chunder Mittra disappeared and has not since been found. These weapon and ammunition passed into the hands of anarchists and have been used in dacoity and theft cases. Two pistols and 23,200 rounds of ammunition have since been recovered. Ten persons were prosecuted in connection with this theft and conspiracy to steal, of whom six were discharged and four convicted and sentenced to two years' rigorous imprisonment each during the current year. The question as to what action was to be taken against the firm responsible for this large loss of arms and ammunition was still under the consideration of the Government at the close of the year.

The remaining arms and ammunition are variously disbursed on the day of the heist itself. As planned, Haridas drives the cart to an open field near Kanti Mukherjee's iron warehouse, close to Malanga Lane. On Bipin Behari's orders, three rebels—Satish Dey, Basanta Das and Jagat Gupta—meet the cart, dressed as coolies. With warlike efficiency, they load the cases into a few hired carts and transport them to the house of Bhujanga Bhushan

Dhar at 39 Jelepara Lane. Well into the night, the cache of pistols and bullets is transferred to newly bought steel trunks, and the wooden cases burnt afterwards.

Once again under Bipin Behari's supervision, the state-of-the-art Mausers and abundant ammunition are distributed among various groups over the next few days. Part of the supply reaches Bagha Jatin, who has, quite literally, become a source of terror for the British government. And so the stage is set for the now legendary battle on 9 September 1915, on the banks of the Buribalam in Orissa (now Odisha), between Bagha Jatin and his four lieutenants on the one hand, and a huge British force on the other. Using a few of the plundered Mausers and ammunition, Bagha Jatin, Chittopriyo Roychoudhury, Jyotish Pal, Manoranjan Sengupta and Niren Dasgupta are determined to fight to the end, no matter how unequal the combat. Surrender, however, becomes inevitable once the ammunition runs out.

'We're running out of bullets...'

'Right... How much longer?'

As is widely known, Chittopriyo succumbs to his injuries on the spot, and an injured Bagha Jatin the day after, in hospital. Jyotish is awarded fourteen years of rigorous imprisonment, while Manoranjan and Niren are sentenced to death by hanging.

By September of 1917, the police have recovered thirty-one Mauser pistols and nearly 27,000 bullets from various parts of Bengal. However, statistics reveal the damage that has already been suffered by the British. Using the stockpile of Mausers and bullets, revolutionaries have caused twenty-seven deaths and forty-four injuries in a total of forty-four political attacks in Bengal.

The daring, successful arms heist acted as a spark in the already simmering atmosphere of sedition. The backbone of the heist was

Habu Mitra, who remained untraced despite the police's untiring efforts. Many of the conspirators, including Srish and Anukul, were arrested and sentenced, but Habu steadfastly avoided capture. What happened to him? Where did he run to?

The records state that he caught the *Darjeeling Mail* out of Calcutta on the night of the robbery. Having reached Churigram in Rangpur (now in Bangladesh), he remained under cover for a while at the home of revolutionary Dr Surendra Bardhan, who, to keep him safe from the police, handed him over to the custody of the Rava tribe of Goalpara, Assam. Sometime later, Dr Bardhan learned that Habu had started for Manipur, after which point there is no documented trace of him. According to Dr Bardhan's own writings, 'I feel, given Habu's immense courage, it is quite possible he tried to flee the country, and also possible that he met with a misadventure.'

Unfortunately, no known image of Habu Mitra exists.

The saga of the freedom movement in Bengal is full of names that history has lovingly handed down. The likes of Khudiram Bose, Prafulla Chaki, Bagha Jatin, Benoy–Badal–Dinesh have deservingly received history's accolades. Nevertheless, an observation of history as found in the Kolkata Police's repository makes it seem as though these legends have also, occasionally, been mercifully judged by time.

There were so many more like Habu Mitra who were unknown and unsung, whose contributions to the struggle were immeasurable, and who never quite found a place among 'the many lives that were sacrificed', or 'the rebel friends who coloured with their blood'. The secondary cast of characters has remained neglected by history. There are no busts in their honour, no colourful celebrations of their births and deaths.

Still, remember them. You must.

Bipin Behari Ganguly

Narendranath Bhattacharya (M.N. Roy)

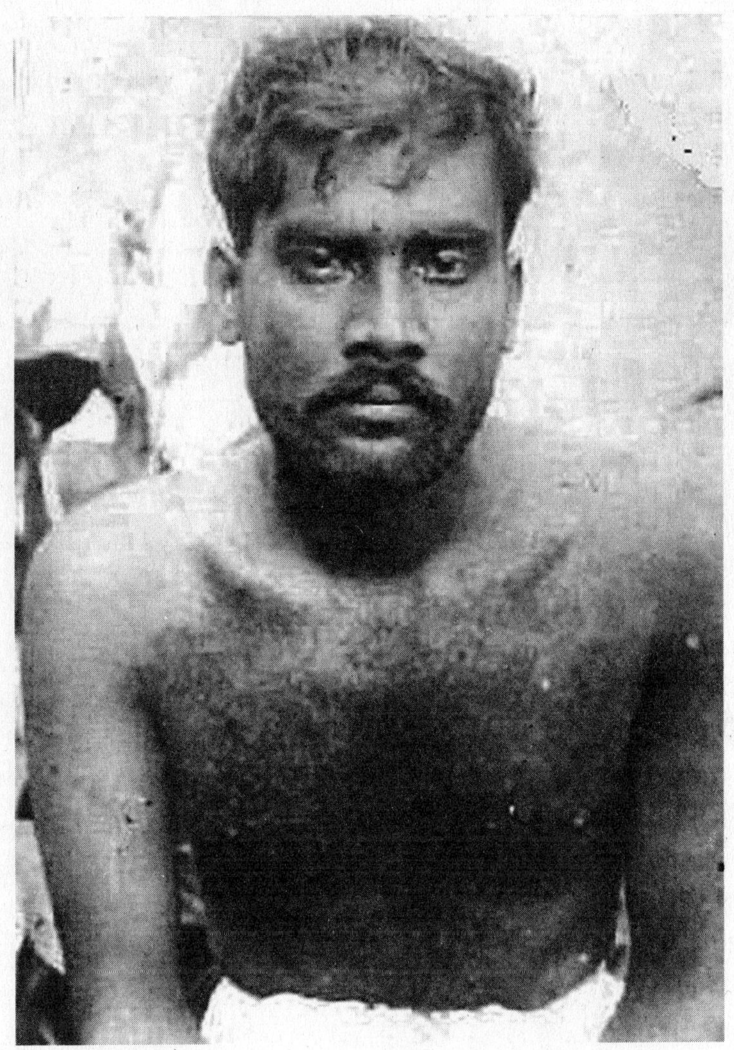

Srish Chandra Pal

Anukul Chandra Mukherjee

Haridas Dutta

Mauser pistol without butt for use as a pistol

Mauser pistol with butt which can be used as a rifle

Chapter 5

THE FALL GUY: RADHA CHARAN PRAMANIK

'THIS ISN'T RIGHT, what you're doing. This is suicide.'

Lying on the bed, the young man tries to smile in reply.

'Why do all of you keep saying this? I've told you I'm not seeing a doctor.'

'And you think that's that? You'll kill yourself and we'll just have to watch? How will the fight go on if you become this emotional?'

His body visibly in the effortless grasp of excruciating pain, the young man nevertheless sticks to his stand.

'Death is better than accepting their charity. I don't want it. They'll think before treating us like animals next time…this is a fight too…'

'The hell they will…in the medical report, they'll simply mention that you refused treatment.'

'Let them write whatever they want, please, just don't force me to do anything…'

Once again, his body seems to crumple in agony. Standing around helplessly, his friends wonder whether they have any option other than counting down the hours to the inevitable end.

'Sir, to your right...'

'What?'

'There...'

The excitement in his junior colleague's voice alerts the uniformed officer. Glancing swiftly to his right, he seems thunderstruck, both by astonishment and the delight of an unexpected gift. This is a bolt from the blue, indeed. Realizing how foolish it will be to waste even a second, he cautions his bodyguard.

'Be careful, Banbehari. We must take him, he's a prize catch. He's run rings around us. Give me cover when I hold the revolver to his head.'

'Sir.'

'He's a rascal, remember. Dangerous. Shoot as soon as you see any sign of trouble. No need to wait for orders. Clear?'

'Right, Sir.'

'And Shiuprasad, you'll be a few steps behind me...'

'Ji, Sahab.'

Moving swiftly, the uniformed officer walks up to within a few paces of the unmindful young man as he stands near Hedua in north Calcutta. Danger strikes before he can take his revolver out of its holster at his waist. The renowned officer from Lalbazar cannot even have imagined the events about to unfold.

Neither could the handful of residents out at this hour have dreamt that they would witness what is about to happen at 6.30 on a blameless winter morning when the city is turning over for another snooze, not even stretching its limbs yet.

'A little faster, Sardarji...'

One of the riders urges the Sikh taxi driver on. Slightly annoyed, the driver presses down harder on the accelerator. He has been hearing the same instruction every second minute since the ride began, '*Faster!' Why are these people in such a tearing hurry? What harm can a five-minute delay do*?

As soon as they get to the Garden Reach crossing, one of the riders orders in a low voice, 'Stop here.'

A hackney carriage approaches them from the opposite direction, moving very slowly. The sight of it seems to really stir up the occupants of the taxi. 'Stop, Sardarji!'

Why are they asking him to stop here? The driver is unable to hide his curiosity.

'Here? Weren't you supposed to go further?'

He earns a rebuke for his troubles.

'Don't ask questions. Stop the taxi in front of that carriage, quickly...'

He has begun to suspect something amiss, but has little choice. Revolvers tucked into waists have suddenly made their way into the hands of his passengers. As he catches sight of the firearms, the taxi driver obeys in terrified silence.

It is the first half of 1915. The heat of World War I is making itself felt in the activities of Bengal's revolutionaries too. Like-minded freedom fighters who have declared war on the British Raj are keen to approach the mighty Germany for help, led by Bagha Jatin. The successful heist in 1914 of a consignment of arms belonging to R.B. Rodda & Co., near Dalhousie, has fired up the revolutionaries as much as it has strengthened the government's determination to crack down on them with greater force. Searches and arrests are on in full swing, armies of spies are working harder than ever, the powers that be at Lalbazar have declared war too unwilling to cede an inch of ground to the enemy.

Very soon, the likes of Bagha Jatin, Bipin Behari Ganguly, Rashbehari Bose and other rebel leaders realize the complete impossibility of keeping alive the fight against an all-powerful national government, based solely on emotion and passion. They need to broaden their organizational base, and need a regular supply of weapons. The dual needs can only be met with increased funds, which they must raise.

The tacitly acknowledged commander of all of Bengal's armed freedom fighters, Bagha Jatin holds a series of secret meetings. His message is unambiguous: in the fight against the power of the Crown, no risk is too great. And having reviewed the situation, he accords the greatest priority to a quick acquisition of funds, at any cost.

Which is all very well, but where will the funds come from?

It is the afternoon of 12 February 1915. An ancient, rickety hackney carriage is making its slow, unsteady way to Garden Reach. Its occupants are a junior employee of Messrs Bird & Co. and two guards.

Ten jute sacks filled with money belonging to the company are also among the occupants. The carriage's destination is the South Union Mill in Badartala, where employees of the jute mill await their salary. The mild winter afternoon sun is in keeping with the snail's pace of the swaying carriage, lulling the passengers into a state of lethargy.

Near the Garden Reach crossing, however, all lethargy vanishes. Their way is blocked by a taxi, driven by a frightened-looking middle-aged Sikh, who only moments earlier has received a tongue-lashing: 'Don't ask questions. Stop the taxi in front of that carriage, quickly...'

Four young men leap out of the taxi, each holding a revolver. As though by magic, three more men appear from nowhere, having lain in wait nearby all this while. The carriage is forced to a standstill, and in the next ten minutes, the employee and guards are held at gunpoint, the sacks of money are unloaded from the carriage and loaded into the taxi, the driver is forced out, and the group of seven drive away in the vehicle.

The sacks are not exactly lightweight: 340 notes totalling Rs 3,400, one rupee silver coins worth Rs 13,000, 50-paise coins worth Rs 940. The rest of the money is in small change, four annas and two annas, and all of it totals Rs 18,400.

Bound for the southern suburb of Baruipur, the taxi speeds along, until one of its tyres stops working near Rajpur. Nevertheless, it is driven to Subuddhipur, and the money is finally packed into two trunks bought in Baruipur.

The car is entrusted to a local resident, who is told that the passengers will return with tools to repair it from Calcutta. The trunks are loaded into two horse carriages hired at Baruipur station. The route now takes a turn towards the Sundarbans, to the north. Thence by boat to Pechuakhali, and an undercover hiatus of two days, and finally onwards to Taki at 11.00 a.m. on 15 February.

Two more trunks are bought so that the loot may be equally distributed. Taking several roundabout routes, the group of seven reach Patipukur station at around 8.00 p.m., from where three hired cars transport them to the hideout at 20 Fakir Chand Mitra

Street. The one thing left to do is disburse the funds to various revolutionary outfits, following Bagha Jatin's instructions.

Within a mere ten days, before the police have had time to get over their bewilderment at the suddenness of the Garden Reach raid, the robbers stage a repeat. Once again, they are in a vehicle, and the target this time is the prosperous rice mill owner Lalitmohan Vrindavan Shah, a resident of Chawal Patti in Beleghata, and a known British sympathizer. On 22 February, at around 9.30 p.m., a group of six or seven, carrying pistols, breaks into Shah's house. The cashier in an adjacent office chamber is shot below the waist when he refuses to hand over the keys to the cash box. In just about five minutes, Rs 22,000 is cleaned up, a pistol held to Shah's head.

The group involved in the Garden Reach heist was mentored by Narendranath Bhattacharya, one of Bagha Jatin's highly trusted lieutenants, who became famous as M.N. Roy in later years. At various stages of planning and implementation, Atul Krishna Ghosh, Saroj Bhushan Das, Fanindra Nath Chakraborty, Biman Chandra Ghosh, Rajanikanta Basu, Prakash Chandra Basu, Bijoy Krishna Ghosh, Gopal Chandra Dutta, Manoranjan Sengupta, Niren Dasgupta and others were companions on the journey. The Beleghata incident saw the active participation of Chittopriyo Roychoudhury, apart from Fanindra–Manoranjan–Niren, and more than one rebel devoted to Bagha Jatin.

To come back to our story, it is inevitable that a rattled Lalbazar will strike back with all its might, and on the evening of 18 February, Narendranath is arrested near Fariapukur at the Shyambazar five-point crossing. On 24 February, the police raid the house at Fakir Chand Mitra Street where the revolutionaries had stayed on the night of 15 February, with their trunks of money. A Mauser pistol and a few cartridges which formed part of the Rodda company loot are recovered from the house. Four revolutionaries—Hiralal Biswas, Niranjan Das, Patit Paban Ghosh and Radha Charan Pramanik—are arrested.

Both missions are led by Inspector Suresh Chandra Mukherjee, a particular favourite of the Lalbazar top brass at the time. Remarkably courageous, and the operator of an enviable spy network, his presence on most of the city's anti-revolutionary missions was almost mandatory. Simultaneously, he was becoming known for his torture of the rebels post their arrest. Once Narendranath and his comrades are arrested, Bagha Jatin decides that Suresh can no longer be allowed to live, and the script for a murder is written, to be eventually enacted on Cornwallis Street, a stone's throw from Hedua.

28 February 1915.

The convocation ceremony of Calcutta University is just days away, with the viceroy scheduled to attend. And so Suresh arrives at the break of dawn to supervise preparations. With him are Sub-inspector Banbehari Mukherjee and long-time bodyguard Shiuprasad. As he scrutinizes the viceroy's route, his attention is attracted by Banbehari's low voice.

'Sir, to your right...'

'What?'

Looking to his right, Suresh's nerves are suddenly wide awake. For months, he has been looking high and low for that young man standing there so nonchalantly. Chittopriyo! Chittopriyo Roychoudhury, one of Bagha Jatin's most faithful shadows. Truly a bolt from the blue!

'We must take him, he's a prize catch. He's run rings around us. Give me cover when I hold the revolver to his head.'

'Sir.'

Walking swiftly up to Chittopriyo with his companions, Suresh grabs the young man's collar. An instant later, Chittopriyo whips out a revolver from his waist and shoots. Destiny intervenes, and the bullet misfires.

Scattered around the area, closely watching the unfolding drama, are Chittopriyo's fellow rebels, Manoranjan, Niren and Naren Ghosh Choudhury. Sensing trouble, they run up to the scene, and Naren fires at Suresh from behind. The aim is impeccable, and Suresh collapses. As he lies on the pathway, multiple bullets find their way into him.

Suresh's companions try resistance, in vain. Shiuprasad takes a bullet to the thigh, while Banbehari narrowly escapes the bullet meant for him. In front of the few stunned onlookers out for their morning constitutional, the quartet makes its escape, shooting all the while. Operation successful.

Suresh, who dies on the way to the hospital, could not have known that the rebels had very deliberately placed Chittopriyo in his line of vision that morning. They knew that Suresh, bound to try and capture a revolutionary who was near the top of the police's most wanted list, would come within striking distance, and fall victim to a surprise attack. The oppressor would not be given even a chance at self-defence.

Robbers posing as passengers in a car are certainly a unique addition to Calcutta's crime landscape—that too, twice in a space of ten days. And before the aftermath has worn off, the murder of a policeman in broad daylight. What next? Where and when?

To say that the higher-ups at Lalbazar are shivering in their boots would perhaps be an exaggeration, but it may unhesitatingly be said that the twin blows of the robberies and an officer's murder have raised uncomfortable questions about Calcutta Police's source network and its crime-controlling abilities. Indeed, senior officers are forced to submit innumerable explanations for the police's failure to the government.

The blueprint for retaliation is drawn up during a series of meetings between the commissioner and top-ranking officers. It is decided that one way to stem the tide of 'taxi dacoities' or 'motor dacoities' is to completely overhaul the city's surveillance procedures. Thus, for the first time in the history of Calcutta Police, drop gates or barriers made of bamboo or iron are placed at prominent thoroughfares, where vehicles are stopped and searched as per the new regulations. In modern policing jargon, the practice is known as nakabandi (checkpoints/roadblocks).

The existing patrolling system undergoes radical changes too. Customized vehicles carrying armed police personnel, variously designated as Armoured Car and Flying Squad, begin round-the-clock patrolling from north to south, east to west. Entry and exit points in the city are now manned by armed guards. The spotlight is particularly on north and east Calcutta, the parts of the city where rebel hideouts are predominantly concentrated. Random stop-and-search exercises, involving random citizens and vehicles, are conducted in areas such as Chitpur, Tala, Belgachhia, Maniktala, Narkeldanga and Howrah Bridge. Alarms are installed in several thanas.

The annual police report of 1915 clearly indicates the role played by the twin robberies and the Hedua murder in revamping the city's surveillance system.

> Political Crime – The present year has been marked by an outbreak of serious political crime of a new form, namely motor-car dacoities, and in addition here have been three cases of murder by the anarchist party, two of the victims being police officers. Special preventive measures in the shapes of patrols, alarms and traffic barriers were taken to deal with this particular form of crime, and the activities of the anarchist party have been checked by arrests in Calcutta and the neighbourhood under the Defence of India Act.
>
> The Special Branch assisted the local police in the investigation of 17 cases during the year. Details of the most important are given below:
>
> Garden Reach Taxi Dacoity Case—On the 12th February 1915 at 2 P.M. a sircar and two durwans of Messrs. Bird & Co., Calcutta, were conveying Rs. 18,000 in cash in a ticca gharry to the South Union Mill when their gharry was stopped in Garden Reach by four armed Bengalis in a taxi. The occupants of the gharry were compelled to make over their cash under threats of being shot and the dacoits then decamped in the taxi throwing out the chauffeur as they drove off. They were eventually traced through the Sundarbans back to Calcutta and four of them were arrested in the Northern Town, one with a loaded Mauser pistol but no property was recovered. Two of the accused were subsequently put on trial, one being convicted and sentenced to seven years' rigorous imprisonment and the other acquitted. The chauffeur, a Sikh employee of the

Indian Taxi Company, was an accomplice and has since been interned in jail.

Belliaghatta Motor Dacoity—On the 22nd February 1915 at about 09.30 P.M. a band of 15 Bengali youths armed with pistols attacked the counting house of Lalit Mohan Brindabun Shah at 25, Chaulpatti Road, Belliaghatta, in motor cars and looted Rs. 19,000 in Government Currency notes. The cashier was wounded by a revolver shot and taxi driver shot dead by the dacoits. The numbers of the stolen notes could not be correctly given by the complainant and he and his servants declared their inability to identify any of the dacoits, so it was impossible to get evidence to prosecute. The taxi used, together with a Mauser pistol and ammunition was found subsequent to the dacoity in a lane near Circular Road and latter [*sic*] enquiries have given a clue to the gang who committed this crime, 5 of whom have been interned.

Cornwallis Street Murder Case—On the 28th February at 06.30 A.M. Sub-Inspector Suresh Chandra Mukherjee of the Special Branch was shot dead [and] his orderly was severely wounded in Cornwallis Street by three Bengali youths, Chittapriya Roychoudhury, Narendra Das and Manoranjan Sen. The Sub-Inspector had just arrested the first-named who was being sought for. All the accused absconded after the commission of the crime and were not traced until November when they were captured by the Balasore Police.

The trial of those arrested in the Garden Reach and Beleghata cases begins. Released on interim bail, Narendranath turns fugitive, and Lalbazar can never reach him again. The four arrested from Fakir Chand Mitra Street are initially booked under the Arms Act. In an act of vengeance, however, the police also frame two of them—Patit Paban Ghosh and Radha Charan Pramanik—in the Garden Reach robbery case, though they are in no way involved.

Patit Paban, out on bail under the Arms Act, now once again finds himself arrested for robbery. This causes a fair amount of concern among Bagha Jatin and the rebel leadership. Patit is a highly active soldier of the freedom movement, with a significant role to play in several upcoming armed revolutionary operations. With him in prison, these operations will be disrupted. There has to be some way to keep him free.

The way is suggested by the defence lawyer. Following a series of discussions with the prosecution lawyers, he announces that the only way to get Patit out of this case is if his co-accused, Radha Charan, submits a statement in court admitting to his own role in the robbery. The catch is Radha Charan will then be sentenced to the far harsher punishment of seven years' rigorous imprisonment instead of the two years he was originally getting under the Arms Act.

Such trivialities, however, have never bothered rebels exhilarated by the ideal of freeing the nation. Radha Charan gladly agrees to admit to his non-existent crime, and is duly sentenced to seven years in prison. Patit walks free.

Born in Madaripur of Faridpur district (now in Bangladesh), Radha Charan (1885–1917) was a student when, in 1911, he was inspired by the revolutionary Purna Das to join the freedom movement, and from there, to gradually become a dedicated member of Bagha Jatin's Jugantar group.

In the second year of his incarceration at Alipore Central Jail, Radha Charan contracts an eye infection, which gradually leads to a weakening of his vision. When he appeals to the authorities for medical treatment, to which he is entitled as a prisoner, the instant response from an English jailor is a flat refusal. 'What treatment? A murderous robber like him deserves to turn blind,' is the contemptuous observation. Then and there, Radha Charan decides that under no circumstances will he accept any form of medical treatment during his imprisonment.

Not only does his vision steadily decline, he also contracts a serious stomach ailment after a few weeks. Nevertheless, his absolute determination to forgo all medical treatment at the prison hospital cannot be swayed by any amount of pleading from friends and family. As his condition worsens alarmingly, the prison authorities finally take note and, almost as though for the sake of appearance, urge Radha Charan to accept the medication offered to him. Not only do their requests fall on the deaf ears of the thirty-two-year-old rebel, but he signs an undertaking declaring his voluntary refusal to accept treatment. That undertaking is akin to his death warrant.

'Death is better than accepting their charity. I don't want it… this is a fight too…'

It is a two-pronged battle, actually, one against physical ailment and one to preserve self-respect. His defeat in the first was unavoidable, but his martyr's victory in the second has made him immortal.

Countless such battles and sacrifices, by the unnamed and unknown, their stories untold and unheard, were part of Bengal's fiery revolutionary era.

Those stories were written in tears.

Chittopriyo Roychoudhury

Niren Dasgupta

Manoranjan Sengupta

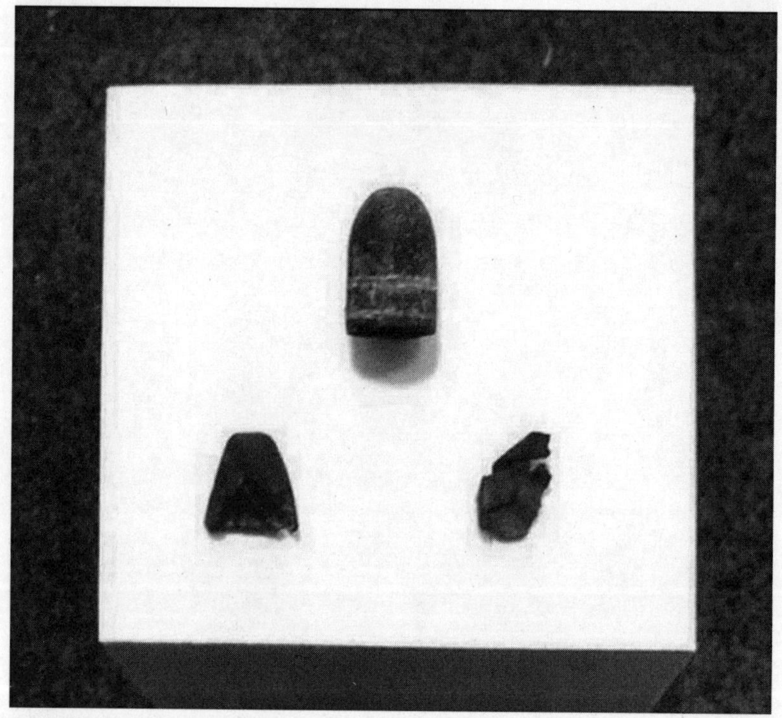

Bullet heads extracted from the body of Inspector Suresh Chandra Mukherjee

Chapter 6

GOAL LINE SAVE: RABINDRANATH TAGORE

HIS EVER-SMILING FACE is a little despondent today, his cheerful banter, which can light up a room, conspicuous by its absence, casting a shadow. The others are troubled: What's wrong? Is he ill? Or is it something else?

The evening's session has proceeded as it usually does. Poet Satyendranath Dutta has been reciting his new works, Dwijendranath Bagchi has been reading poetry criticism from a notebook, Dinendranath Tagore has been breaking into his habitual full-throated songs and Manilal Gangopadhyay has been enthusiastically reading out his differently flavoured stories.

Nonetheless, the man at the centre of it all seems far away, visibly unenthusiastic about letting them hear his new creations, as he normally does. Finally, young police court lawyer Sourindramohan Mukhopadhyay, a devotee of literature, decides to voice the question uppermost in everyone's minds: 'Gurudev, what is it? Are you ill?'

Rabindranath Tagore smiles weakly.

'No…but your Rabi Thakur will never again be able to write as he did…'

The response is shocked and unanimous. 'What?! Why?!'

'The fountain pen he writes with is lost. Nowhere to be found…'

'Oh! Have you looked everywhere?'

'You think I haven't?'

The evening at Jorasanko loses its rhythm. The loss of his favourite pen has clearly taken Rabindranath far away from the literary session, and music and literature wilt in the face of his indifference.

Two months later. Loud yells of pain ring out of a thana.

'Never again, Huzoor (Sir)! See, I'm twisting my ears myself!'

The officer-in-charge of Jorasanko thana, Boro Babu, listens. And then bellows, 'Shut up! You say the same thing whenever you're caught! Enough of your nose pinching and ear twisting! You'll die but never change!'

This fetches silence from the floor, where the thief is kneeling, a rope tied around his waist. His face bears physical evidence of a recent and generous thrashing, which he has had to digest. What choice does he have? This new Boro Babu has made it almost impossible for him to continue 'business' as usual. Heaven knows how he seems to guess his every move in advance.

Two months ago, this same officer had arrested him from Belgachhia. And this time, from a relative's home in Tala, complete with loot. He thought he had given himself enough time after being granted bail the last time before he resumed 'operations', so the police wouldn't be suspicious.

It had been going so well. A lock broken in one house on a silent night, stuff removed cleverly from another during a lazy afternoon. But no, he had to go and get caught! And they said policemen were always being transferred. *Why wasn't this one going away? How long had he been posted at this thana*?

His musings are interrupted by a stick descending hard on his back.

'Please, Huzoor, no more!'

'You think I'm done with you? Tell us what you've stolen from whom, and be quick, or I'll beat the skin off your back!'

A large cache of stolen goods has been assembled on a table. The haul includes a range of objects: clothes, jewels, utensils, watches, gold buttons, pens, even inkpots.

'Huzoor…that one's from a two-storey house near Kolootola… that one from the doctor's chamber next to Phol Potti (fruit market)…this one…'

Boro Babu grimly notes down every detail. Once the list is done, he orders his subordinate, 'Ask for the car, we're leaving. Get this scoundrel into the car as well. Oi, you! Up!'

A constable shoves the prisoner into the vehicle by the scruff of his neck. Boro Babu settles into the front seat. The driver's questioning glance elicits the brisk response: 'Kolootola first, then Phol Potti, then…'

In 1918, the year in which this account is set, the police court operated within the Lalbazar precincts, in the red brick, three-storey building adjoining the western end of Bentinck Street. Today, it has been replaced by the Traffic Department and various offices of the Reserve Force.

Every floor was dedicated to one or another of the court's numerous activities. In the ground-floor offices sat the clerks, the orderly bar library was on the first floor, and the second and third floors housed the presidency magistrate's court, as well as the office of the public prosecutor, and the courts of the fourth and fifth magistrates. The bustle of lawyers coming and going, and the buzz of arguments and counterarguments, formed the lifeblood of the police court, the same court that witnessed many a trial by fire during the turbulent era of India's freedom movement.

Of course, the flag bearers of that movement are not the subjects of this chapter. No, this time, we look back to a completely different narrative, at the heart of which sits the man who is part of every breath we take: Rabindranath Tagore.

Remember the young lawyer Sourindramohan? Determined not to work for the British government, right from his student days, he has dreamt of spending his life in the dedicated pursuit of literature. However, his dream has been subdued by none other than Rabindranath who, extremely fond as he is of the young man, has persuaded him to make the law his profession, and literature his passion.

In the court, Sourindramohan suddenly spots Gopal Babu rushing toward him, waving a piece of paper. Gopal is part of Rabindranath's household staff, an odd-job man. His master trusts him implicitly. Sourindramohan is a little taken aback at his presence in the court at such an odd hour, almost mid-afternoon. Is something the matter with Rabindranath?

'It's you I've come to see. He's in trouble…look here…'

Panting, Gopal thrusts the paper into Sourindramohan's hand. And even a quick glance is enough to render him speechless.

A summons from the court for Rabindranath Tagore! It bears the signature of the third Presidency Magistrate Anis-uz-Zaman Khan, and the official seal too. In a nutshell, Rabindranath has been ordered to appear in such and such court on such and such date to testify in the matter of a theft under Section 379 of the Indian Penal Code.

'But what has been stolen? What *is* all this?' asks Sourindramohan, once he has calmed down a little.

Gopal clears matters. 'It's his fountain pen. He lost it a couple of months ago.'

'Yes, yes, I remember. He told us about it.'

'Well, it wasn't lost. It was stolen. And the thief has been caught.'

'And...?'

Boro Babu is still making his rounds, with the thief still trapped in the vehicle. Sheepishly, the thief points out the scenes of his crimes. Having covered Kolootola and Phol Potti, the car enters a lane.

'Which house? Come on!'

Quick to note the anger in Boro Babu's voice, the thief babbles, 'Just a little bit further...'

'How much?'

'Right there...this one, this one, Huzoor...'

The vehicle stops in front of the house in question, with Boro Babu thunderstruck. It takes him a full minute to recover, upon which he very nearly begins thrashing the thief again.

'Are you absolutely sure? This house?'

'Oh yes, this is the one...I took the pen one afternoon when there was nobody around...'

'And you found no other house? There are so many here, almost all of them deserted in the afternoon, and you had to go and steal from this one? This one?'

The thief is stupefied by a stinging slap to his face. Why is Boro Babu so angry? Who lives in this house? Some raja maharaja? Someone even more important? Since when have such details ever concerned a thief on the job?

Incidentally, the occupant of the house is pacing his balcony at that very moment. Surprised to learn that Boro Babu of Jorasanko thana has asked for a word, he descends to the lower floor. The police? Here?

'Gurudev, I'm truly sorry for this trouble. I had no choice but to come and see you.'

Rabindranath looks at him, silent but curious.

As Boro Babu takes out a fountain pen, however, the Bard of Bengal is almost incoherent with childlike glee.

'Here it is! My pen! The pen I write with! I lost it, you know… couldn't find it anywhere. You did though! You found it! Where did you find it? Who took it?'

Having taken down Rabindranath's brief statement in his notebook, Boro Babu prepares to leave. And the poet can't help asking, 'So when do I get it back?'

Boro Babu's polite reply is that the return will not be immediate.

'There'll be a case in court. And you'll get it back as soon as proceedings are over.'

Crestfallen, Rabindranath listens to Boro Babu's explanation of the legal technicalities—how the pen is 'stolen and recovered' property, how it needs to be identified in court as such and how a judge's written order is required before it can be returned to its rightful owner.

Since he has never had much time for the law and its mumbo-jumbo, Rabindranath asks no further questions. He will simply wait until the court has had its say. His pen has been found, that's all he really cares about.

The sense of relief is short-lived however. A few days later, a constable arrives from Jorasanko thana and hands him the summons to appear in court to testify in the matter of his stolen pen.

Feeling faint at the prospect, Rabindranath sinks into his easy chair and calls for Gopal, asking him to rush to the police court. 'Find Sourin, now. Tell him this summons needs to be stopped immediately. Tell him Rabi Thakur will die of heart failure otherwise. If he can't stop it, tell him he can only come to this house with enough men for a funeral procession.'

Distressed and agitated by Gopal's account, Sourindramohan rushes to the magistrate's chamber, to repeat the story to Anis Sahab, himself a lover of literature and a devoted admirer of Rabindranath. The story leaves him dumbfounded for quite a few minutes. Once he has recovered, he sends for Court Inspector Sarat Kumar Ghosh, and this unfortunate man bears the brunt of Anis Sahab's blazing anger.

'What have you done, Sarat Babu? Have you no sense at all?'

It is Sarat Babu's turn to be dumbfounded. What is he supposed to have done, exactly? Why is the usually courteous and level-headed Anis Sahab so livid?

'What have I done, Sir?'

Anis Sahab practically throws the summons at Sarat Babu.

'Look, look at what you've done! Look! You've summoned Rabindranath Tagore to this court! For the simple theft of a pen! Have you any idea what an insult this is for him?'

'What was I to do, Sir? The only name in the officer's report was that of Rabindranath! What was I to do? He himself identified the pen as his. I had no choice. He has to identify the pen in court. Besides, Sir, the law is the same for everyone. Whether it's Rabindranath or...'

He is furiously interrupted.

'So Rabindranath Tagore is the same as everyone else? Don't you dare teach me the law! Do I know the law any less than you? The law is for mere mortals. There can be only one Rabindranath Tagore. The sky won't collapse if you make an exception for him. Sourindra Babu, the man who has brought this summons here, he must have seen this pen numerous times. Can he identify it?'

Sourindramohan nods. Anis Sahab barks out orders immediately.

'Right, that's it then. Sarat Babu, I'm cancelling the summons with immediate effect. You will issue a fresh summons in the name of the man who has brought Gurudev's message. He can come and testify in court, and identify the pen.'

Once Sarat Babu leaves, Anis Sahab grasps Sourindramohan's hands in his.

'Forgive me my terrible sin, Sourindra Babu. All day, I'm signing one paper after another...it has become so routine that I hardly have a chance to check who the summonses are going out to. Do beg Rabindranath's forgiveness on my behalf. Give him all my respect and tell him I pray for his forgiveness, and that he may please grant me my prayer.'

In his book *Ukiler Diary* (Diary of a Lawyer), Sourindramohan (who was to become the father of the legendary Rabindrasangeet vocalist Suchitra Mitra) has a humorous description of the aftermath of this incident. 'The matter was resolved then and there. Gopal Babu left, and when I went and met Rabindranath after court, he smiled and said, "You've saved Rabi Thakur from an untimely death today. Remember the saying, a friend is with you at the cremation ground as well as in the king's court. A thousand blessings for the friendship you have shown me in the king's court. May glory forever be yours"!'

During their long and fascinating existence, the portals of Lalbazar have been privileged to receive their fair share of illustrious citizens, most of them during the fiery days of India's freedom struggle, either as prisoners, or as witnesses or accused in some case or the other. Undoubtedly, the police headquarters would have been supremely blessed had Rabindranath stepped through its gates. Upon deeper reflection though it is perhaps as well that the case did not reach this ultimate conclusion. The sight of a Nobel laureate, revered the world over, in the witness box to identify a stolen fountain pen would have proved almost unbearably trying.

As they say in football, this was a 'goal line save' indeed.

Rabindranath Tagore

Jorasanko Thakurbari

Dinendranath Tagore

Cover page of Ukiler Diary

Chapter 7

LONE WOLF: GOPIMOHAN SAHA

'MAY I HAVE a pen and paper?'

'Of course. Anything else? Anything you want to eat? We can arrange it.'

The frail, dark young man smiles slightly. 'No, just a pen and paper. I need to write a letter.'

Wordless, the guard leaves to fetch a pen and paper. This boy is to be hanged the day after next. What exactly is he made of?

The standing instruction from the jail authorities for prisoners thus condemned is that all their requests should be met, within reasonable limits. In the past month, this serene boy has captured hearts, to the point where the mind finds it impossible to accept him as a murderer.

He reads a lot, and meditates quietly in front of a small idol of Goddess Kali. He shows no remorse for what he has done, and has made no special requests, despite repeated encouragement. It is impossible to believe that he will be facing the noose in a mere forty-eight hours. For him, today is like any other day; there are no visible signs of inner turmoil, if any. Why isn't he even remotely scared?

'Here, pen and paper. Will this do?'

This time, the smile is radiant.

'Oh absolutely... if this letter could be delivered...'

'We'll take care of that... don't worry.'

Visibly reassured, the young man sits down to write his last letter.

'Dear Ma...'

The huge bungalow is crawling with guards and sentries on watch, guns on display, round-the-clock. Unknown faces are strictly forbidden. The administration spares no trouble in ensuring the security of the man who lives here with his family, the man at the centre of all the activity.

He's a formidable man, a virtual stranger to fear. Rising at the crack of dawn, he sets off on his morning walk unaccompanied by security personnel. At a brisk pace, he emerges from Kyd Street, walks down Park Street and then Chowringhee. His uncompromising approach to physical fitness is a childhood habit, and on some early mornings, the vast greens of the Maidan are witness to a well-built rider and his horse, criss-crossing the expanse.

On other mornings, like today, the agenda is target practice on his spacious terrace, using a revolver and a canvas bearing a life-size drawing of a man armed with a pistol. This is the target, and it is placed at one end of the terrace, while two White men stand side by side, forty metres away, revolvers tucked into their holsters.

This isn't an ordinary, measured, targeted shooting practice. Real-life shootouts hardly offer time for careful aiming and firing. The two men, therefore, focus on recreating reality as far as they can to test their skills, standing with their backs to the target, chatting casually, until one lets out a sudden cry to alert the other.

'There! Fire!'

Instantly, his companion wheels around as fast as he can, whips out his revolver and fires at the target. This goes on for about an hour, accompanied by a painstaking scrutiny of aiming techniques. Shots that don't find the 'killing zone' of head–chest–stomach don't really count. Hitting the lower parts of the body will cause injury, but a fatality, almost never. And so it goes on over and over, the attempt to obliterate the life-size target's chest or thereabouts.

'Let's start afresh, Colson.'

'Right, Charles!'

Meanwhile, a blueprint for murder is being fine-tuned.

'A chance like this will never come again. Gopi, remember, just keep shooting until you're sure the scoundrel is dead.'

Months of hard labour devoted to fact-finding, along with numerous discussions, have given birth to the plan. It is now time to implement it. Closeted in a central Calcutta hideout, rebel leader Anantalal Singha briefs the team before the ultimate assault.

'Just to go over the important points, he leaves Kyd Street at 6.00 in the morning, with a terrier. The attack will happen somewhere between Kyd Street and Chowringhee, either on his way out or way back, whichever is convenient for us.

'Gopimohan has been following him for days now, he knows

exactly what he looks like, he will do the shooting. You'll have a revolver in one hand, a pistol in the other. If Gopi misses, Khoka shoots. Khoka...you'll be standing about 50–60 yards from Gopi.

'If the target tries to escape down Free School Street to the east, I'll shoot. I'll be waiting 70–80 yards from Gopi.

'Khoka will be in European clothes. He'll carry a revolver, obviously, and a time bomb that can be set off in seven seconds with a lotion. I'll carry the same bomb and revolver, and I'll be dressed as a Bengali.

'Gopi will be disguised as a Muslim, with a fez cap and a woollen scarf to hide the scar on his face. If he succeeds, well and good, and if not, Khoka or I will attack. We'll chase and kill the scum no matter where he runs.

'Julu Da, you take the Mauser pistol. You'll be cycling around the area, to help as and when needed. And watch out for the plainclothesmen. They're everywhere.'

Finally, Anantalal pauses for breath, and looks at Gopi.

'Gopi? You can, can't you?'

The seemingly ordinary young man looks straight back at Anantalal as he runs his hands over his revolver, his voice calm but his eyes glittering with excitement.

'You still have doubts? You know I'd risk anything to remove that man from this world. He doesn't have the right to live even a day longer.'

Indeed, the majority of Bengal's armed freedom fighters in those fiery times believed 'that man' had no right to live. Sir Charles

Augustus Tegart, the man whose initials had given rise to the nickname 'Cat', among the revolutionaries.

Born in Northern Ireland, Charles Tegart (1881–1946) was for some time a meritorious student at Trinity College, Dublin. In 1901, he joined the Indian Police (Imperial Police) and was posted to Pataliputra, at a time when Bihar and Orissa were part of Bengal. Transferred to Calcutta in 1906, he joined the Detective Department as acting deputy commissioner. His rise over the next twenty-five years of uninterrupted service with Calcutta Police was proverbially meteoric.

The lion's share of the credit for having established the Special Branch, as well as its infrastructural foundation, goes to Tegart, whose razor-sharp intelligence and indomitable courage were complemented by his exceptional 'source network', not just in Calcutta, but across Bengal. All of this made him virtually unbeatable, and, as far as the contemporary British administration was concerned, almost a legend. Elevated to the post of commissioner of police in 1923, he was the undisputed lord and master of Calcutta Police for eight years.

Tegart remains an immensely controversial personality. A dispassionate, purely professional analysis would label him an asset to any administration, as an officer. Indeed, more than one revolutionary, in whose flesh he was a painful thorn, viewed his efficiency and professional skills with respect. Residents of Calcutta had one particular reason to be grateful to Tegart. He rid Calcutta of its goondas.

In turn, despite his public loathing of the revolutionaries, Tegart was reportedly impressed by some of India's leading freedom fighters in private. 'Had selfless patriots like Bagha Jatin and Aurobindo Ghosh been born in England, they would have had busts built for them in their lifetimes,' he is known to have told those close to him.

He had a keen sense of humour too, Tegart. A story goes that a lady once came to meet him seething about having lost a court case, and wishing to apply for a gun licence.

'Why do you need a gun?' Tegart asked her.

'Why? Well first, I would like to shoot Tegart dead. And then the magistrate who judged my case!'

Tegart smiled in response. 'That is all very well, but you can't have the licence, I'm afraid. We only issue licences to those applicants who declare they will use their guns more than twice!'

Not only did Tegart efficiently deal with the menace of thugs and gangsters in Calcutta, during his long career, he put countless notorious lawbreakers behind bars based on information from his sources, and personally led innumerable highly dangerous missions.

In all fairness, it is necessary to admit that those engaged in maintaining the law and order in a country that has declared a war of independence are rarely accorded the privilege of an objective assessment, forget gratitude. No matter how disagreeable the administration's policies, a government servant is bound to implement them, even if they violate his conscience.

Then why, compared to other British officials of the Raj, has Tegart been singled out for vilification and condemnation? There's a simple answer: driven by boundless ambition, Tegart had no trouble eliminating the divide between the city's petty crooks or feared gangsters and its beloved, patriotic revolutionaries.

Not that he was unaware of the difference between the two, but he made a conscious decision to sacrifice this awareness in order to satisfy his relentless need to earn a place in the government's good books. Not content with simply arresting revolutionaries, he scaled unprecedented heights of cruelty in his treatment of these prisoners, to the point where the merciless torture of enemies of the Crown became part of his very self. He had begun to find new definitions of torture through practise.

Borrowing an idea from iconic poet Michael Madhusudan Dutt, the goal was to eliminate the enemy, never mind the strategy ('*Mari ori pari je koushole*', for those interested in the original Bengali). To use an example, while planning an operation to capture a revolutionary, as Tegart explained the details to his officers, one of the men asked, 'What if he opens fire?'

'Why would you let him? Fire before he does,' was the reply.

'But Sir, say we fire, and he dies. And then we find he wasn't carrying a firearm at all. What then? By law, we can't fire on an unarmed man. We could cite self-defence, but that doesn't apply to an unarmed man. What if there's no firearm?'

'In that case, you are to find one.'

The orders were crystal clear. If there was no weapon, one was to be placed in the corpse's hand or pocket or anywhere else. The case for self-defence would then become irrefutable.

That was Tegart, never one for ethics or morals when it came to countering revolutionaries. Indeed, the target shooting on the terrace of his Kyd Street bungalow while he was commissioner, hints at Tegart's unimaginably deep hatred of Bengal's armed freedom fighters.

'Let's start afresh, Colson.'

'Right, Charles!'

Based on his life, Tegart's wife Catherine wrote a book which never progressed beyond 340 pages of a typed manuscript. Though finally unpublished, the book had a foreword by S.G. Taylor, once Bengal's inspector general of police. Titled *Memoirs of an Indian Policeman*, the book valorized Tegart, and Catherine described the target practice sessions thus: 'He had a life-size sketch of a Bengali assassin, levelling a pistol, made on canvas which was kept on the roof and when another officer (usually Mr Colson, who succeeded him as commissioner) joined in the practice, it was the custom for one or the other of them, while they did the morning exercise, to give a sudden unpremeditated yell; on this, the other had to switch round with his automatic and shoot the canvas gunman in some vital part of his anatomy.'

Inevitably, a man such as Tegart was destined to head the revolutionaries' hit list. Of the multiple plots to assassinate him, one was formed by the rebel quartet of Anantalal Singha, Debendra Chandra Dey (Khoka), after whom D.C. Dey Road in Kolkata's Entally area is named, Gopimohan Saha and Nagendranath Sen (Julu).

'A chance like this will never come again. Gopi, remember, just keep shooting until you're sure the scoundrel is dead.'

Standing on Free School Street at around 6.00 a.m., Anantalal fidgets nervously. Will it all go according to plan? He can see Gopi clearly, in a fez and woollen scarf as planned. Khoka is out of sight. Julu Da must be making the rounds on his bicycle.

He lights a cigarette to ease the tension though there's another purpose at work. Smoking was not common among revolutionaries of the time, and so the highly alert plainclothesmen who line Tegart's early morning route are less likely to be suspicious of a man with a cigarette. Unaccustomed to the habit, Anantalal nearly chokes on the smoke. *How on earth do people swallow this stuff?*

As he waits, Anantalal expects the shots from Gopi's pistol to ring out any minute, and for the enemy to be vanquished. When, though? Time seems to be standing still. Is there a problem?

The worrying answer arrives soon enough in the form of Julu Da, who materializes on his bicycle.

'Back to the house, now. There's been an accident. Khoka has set fire to himself. Mission abandoned.'

Consumed by despair, Anantalal can guess exactly what has happened. The bottle of lotion intended to light the explosive, which Khoka has in his pocket, contains a highly unstable mix of yellow phosphorus and carbon disulphide. If even a few drops have escaped onto Khoka's clothes, the carbon disulphide will have evaporated quickly, leaving only phosphorus, which catches fire as soon as it is exposed to atmospheric oxygen.

And that is indeed what has happened. The sight of a young man in European attire on a Calcutta thoroughfare, his clothes on fire, has stopped passers-by dead in their tracks.

'*Sahab kya hua? Aag kaise lagi?* (What happened, Sahab? How did the fire start?)'

'*Cigarette se lag gayi* (Started from my cigarette)...'

Phosphorus on fire is virtually untameable. Not even water is of much use, since the fire starts up again as soon as the water has dried out, and burns for as long as the phosphorus lasts.

Desperately, Khoka tries to stem the fire using water from a roadside hydrant. He knows there's a bigger disaster waiting to happen if the flames are not subdued quickly. In his trouser pocket is a live bomb stuffed with picric powder, attached to a gun cotton fuse. The moment the fire reaches it, the explosion, and his end, will be instantaneous. Somehow, he manages to extract the bomb and soak it in water. Killing Tegart can come later, he has to save his own life first!

Their operation nipped in the bud, the four gloomy rebels reassemble in their Taltala hideout. Khoka has taken off his still smoking suit and dumped it in a bucket of water. And a furious Anantalal is ranting at him.

'Have you no brains at all? Always careless! Couldn't you keep the bottle in your breast pocket? Your stupidity has ruined everything!'

Julu Da interrupts the tirade.

'Whatever has happened, has happened, no good thinking about it. This is a lesson for us...we will have to be more careful about technical details in future. Khoka nearly died today. Come on, Gopi, cheer up! Don't let this get you down. Tegart isn't going anywhere; we'll have more chances...'

Stone-faced and red-eyed, Gopi doesn't bother to reply. He has stayed awake all night, captivated by the excitement of finally fulfilling his dream. He has been observing Tegart for the past three months, what he looks like, what he wears and when, the way he walks, all of it. And now, their plan has been ruined by simple carelessness. Julu Da says they will have more chances, but Anantalal Da had said yesterday that such a chance would never come again. Who is he to believe? His mind in turmoil, he decides to believe neither. Whatever he has to do, he will do alone. If that means killing Tegart by himself, so be it.

Sure enough, a few days later, Gopi launches his desperate, lone effort, his companions completely in the dark about his intentions.

12 January 1924. It's 7.00 in the morning, perhaps 7.30. Dressed in a white dhoti and baggy khaki shirt, Gopi hovers uncertainly around the Park Street–Chowringhee Road crossing as he has been doing for a few days now, hoping to catch Tegart unawares. But the canny sahab doesn't take a morning walk every day. On the days he does, he chooses a different route to return each time. Besides, the plain-clothes sleuths are never far from him.

All at once, Gopi's senses are jolted awake. Who's the man standing in front of the large Hall & Anderson outlet? The shop is yet to open, but the tall gentleman is running his eyes over the window display.

Sidling closer, one glance at the man's back is enough to convince Gopi. This has to be Tegart! The way he is standing, the brown overcoat, all of it is completely familiar. At last! At last, he has the immensely powerful commissioner of police within his reach. Finishing him off will release shock waves into every pore of the British administration.

Without wasting a moment, Gopi walks up to the gentleman, and hurriedly pulls the trigger. The bullet flies wide. Alerted by the noise, the man tries to turn around, but the second bullet finds its mark. Gopi then unleashes a hail of bullets into the body lying face down on the pavement. He can take no risks. He has to make sure of death.

A crowd has gathered by now, and Gopi takes off running down Park Street. A few pedestrians give chase, as does a taxi. Gopi fires at the latter, and tries to board a moving car that he has stopped. When the driver refuses to allow him in, he fires again, but misses. Finally, he tries to escape on the footboard of a passing horse carriage, but the police have caught up by now. He is captured, along with a large pistol, revolver and forty live cartridges.

Treated to a rough thrashing on the way to Lalbazar, he is escorted straight to the commissioner's chamber. As he enters, the ground seems to shift from beneath Gopi's feet. Hard as it is to believe, there in his chair sits Tegart, in all his glory. The man into whom he just pumped all those bullets in full public view.

Tegart smiles sardonically at the stunned revolutionary.

'So you thought you'd killed Charles Tegart?'

Soon enough, Gopi realizes the enormity of his mistake. The Tegart lookalike he has killed was an innocent Englishman. His name was Ernest Day, an official of a private firm, who died on his way to a hospital. Tegart, obviously, is alive and very well. Kicking, as they say.

Feeling dizzy, Gopi sinks into a chair, his hands covering his face. How could such a huge error have happened? He has just killed an innocent man, while Tegart has escaped without a scratch, again.

The inevitable headline in the next day's paper reads, 'Mistaken Identity Saves Tegart'. A Bengali paper comes up with, 'Providence Saves Sir Charles Tegart's Life. Brutal Slaying of Mr Ernest Day at Chowringhee. Youth Named Gopinath [*sic*] Saha Arrested on the Spot'.

Tegart, who appears to be destiny's child, was to be a target throughout his career. Either a bomb thrown at his car would narrowly miss its mark, or he wouldn't turn up for a scheduled appearance at the last moment, having received information that armed rebels were lying in wait.

On 25 August 1930, as he was on his way to Lalbazar at around 11.00 in the morning, revolutionaries Dinesh Chandra

Majumdar and Anuja Charan Sengupta hurled a bomb at his car near Dalhousie. Exploding as it landed to the left of the car, the bomb missed its target by inches. Anuja was killed on the spot by another explosive concealed in his pocket, while Dinesh tried to escape, in vain.

Nominated to the Secretary of State's Indian Council, Tegart left Calcutta in 1931, leaving behind him a permanent sense of regret among Bengal's revolutionaries at their failure to end his life.

There was no way out for Gopi. The death sentence was predestined. Having suffered unspeakable torture during his imprisonment, he had this to say at the end of his trial on 16 February, as the sentence of death by hanging was read out in the court of Sessions Judge Pearson: 'I wished to kill Tegart. The fact that I killed an innocent man fills me with eternal regret. I beg the forgiveness of his family. But Tegart shall not be forgiven. I am certain that one among my patriotic comrades will kill the tyrant commissioner, and complete the task I leave unfinished, taking far more care than I have in committing the act.'

Hanging day was to be March 1924. And thus was added another name to the long list of 'those who sang the song of life on the stage of death'; that of Gopimohan Saha, the young man from Hooghly after whom a bridge was named in Srirampur.

The intense reaction to his hanging came not just from Bengal or eastern India, but all over the country. On 2 June 1924, at the Regional Congress Conference in Sirajganj (in modern-day Bangladesh), Chittaranjan Das or Deshbandhu as he was popularly called, proposed a motion paying tribute to Gopi's ultimate sacrifice. Given the Congress's hitherto firm adherence to non-violence, this seeming 'growth of terrorist influence' within the party caused the British administration to sit up and take note. In a confidential report titled 'Brief Note on the Alliance of Congress with Terrorism in Bengal', the Intelligence Branch in Bengal stated:

> Gopi Saha proposal passed. Growth of terrorist influence within the Congress.
>
> In 1924, the extremist members of the Swarajya Party supported the nomination of Subhas Chandra Bose as chief executive officer of the Corporation, and it is to be noted that ever since his appointment to the post, a large number of Corporation jobs have been awarded to terrorists.
>
> At the Sirajganj Congress Conference, Mr C.R. Das with help from his terrorist supporters, got his Hindu–Muslim Pact proposal passed, and in exchange, pushed through the condemnable proposal praising Gopi Saha, the killer of Mr Day. This is a direct encouragement to the youth of Bengal to follow in the killer's footsteps.'

Pro-government English newspapers raised a hue and cry over the proposal praising Gopi passed by the regional Congress. How could the same Congress, which condemned terrorism, accord the status of a martyr to the killer of an innocent citizen at its regional conference? Accusations of duplicity from the government were inevitable.

Deshbandhu fielded all questions head on. The form in which the proposal was published in the media read thus: 'Although eschewing all kinds of violence and accepting the character and basic principle of non-violence, this conference makes known its respect for Gopimohan Saha for the noble self-sacrifice which he, bearing in mind a high and noble ideal, has made for the preservation of the interests of the motherland.'

In other words, 'This conference is against all forms of violence and believes in the ideals of non-violence. Nonetheless, we pay tribute to Gopimohan Saha for his heroic self-sacrifice, behind which lies his desire to protect his country's interests.'

Deshbandhu declared that the original proposal having been written in Bengali, an inaccurate translation had sent out a misleading message. His own translation of the original was: 'This conference, while denouncing (or dissociating itself from) violence (every kind of himsa) and adhering to the principle of non-violence, appreciates Gopimohan Saha's ideal of self-sacrifice, misguided though that is, in the best interest of the country, and expresses its respect for his self-sacrifice.'

Once again, in other words, all that the original Bengali proposal said was: 'This conference condemns all forms of violence (and is committed to maintaining a distance from violence) and believes in the principle of non-violence. Though Gopimohan strayed from these principles in the interests of the nation, this conference still believes his self-sacrifice praiseworthy and pays tribute to him.'

Deshbandhu's explanation infuriated Tegart, and he privately fumed about how it was mere wordplay and, in reality, accolade wrapped in criticism.

A few weeks after Gopi's hanging, a typed notice arrived for Tegart in the post.

BANDE MATARAM

Notice

The public is hereby informed that the Bengal Revolutionary Council has passed a resolution of a campaign of ruthless assassination of police officers. Anyone in any way actively or passively putting obstruction to our comrade when in action or retiring or helping the government of this country as by taking brief from the government or giving evidence in favour of the prosecution, etc. when such comrade is in the hands of the government, or inciting the government to take repressive measures shall be considered as doing acts highly prejudicial to the best interest of our country and from the moment any such action taken by anyone, he shall be considered as condemned to be dispatched forthwith.

PRESIDENT-IN-COUNCIL, RED BENGAL

The final twist in the tale followed a heated debate about the party's official stance on the Gopi issue within the All India Congress Committee. Deshbandhu led the arguments in Gopi's favour, while prominent among those against was Mahatma Gandhi, devoted as always to the creed of non-violence. Ultimately, Deshbandhu's proposal was defeated by the thinnest of margins. Stunned by the number of votes in favour of Gopi's actions, Gandhi was forced to acknowledge the questionable nature of his win, forced to declare himself 'defeated and humbled'.

Two days before his death, using the pen and paper obtained from a prison guard at Presidency Jail, Gopimohan wrote his last letter to his mother, the summary of which reads:

Dear Ma,

Pray to the Almighty that every household in India is blessed to have a mother like you, and that they all give birth to children like your Gopi, who will unthinkingly sacrifice their lives for the sake of their country.

Yours affectionately,
Gopi

What else remains to be said? Or written?

Gopimohan Saha

Mahatma Gandhi

Nagendranath Sen (Julu Sen)

Anantalal Singha

Anuja Charan Sengupta

Dinesh Chandra Majumdar

Chapter 8

THE IMMORTAL TRIO: BENOY-BADAL-DINESH

THE HIT ISN'T point-blank. But the aim is unerring. The bullet travels fifteen metres to pierce his body. He falls face first, and doesn't get up again. The second bullet misses the mark, finding the second target's shoulder, instead of his chest. As he sinks to the ground, his hand pressed to his wound, he yells at the armed guards, 'There he is! Get him!'

One of their bosses lies on the ground, clearly lifeless. The other has a shoulder injury. By the time the stupefied guards come to their senses, the young assassin, in a simple dhoti and vest, is quite a long way away, moving like the proverbial lightning. The chase, hampered by dense crowds of people, is frantic, but fruitless.

The dense crowds are an everyday affair. These are the premises of the Dhaka Medical School and Hospital, besieged by an endless stream of patients from surrounding districts. Doctors struggle to contain them, ambulances dash in and out, and the stretcher-bearers are kept forever busy. Add to that the hordes of cheerful, boisterous medical students, and you get the picture.

So the young man is lost in the crowds, leaving behind him a deed that the British administration finds hard to even imagine, and which makes waves among supporters of India's armed freedom struggle across the length and breadth of the country.

The assassin's anonymity is short-lived, however. His name and photograph are discovered easily, and thousands of 'Wanted' posters are distributed, bearing the promise of a monetary reward should anyone supply further information. The fugitive's name features in large, bold letters.

Benoy Krishna Basu.

Alipore Central Jail
Calcutta
June 18, 1931

Boudi,

That was a long letter you wrote. No life ends before its time. God calls us to Him only once we have done whatever we were supposed to do, never before.

You might remember the way I used to make a doll dance, using your hair. The doll would come and sing, 'Why do you call, Mohan Dhuli?' Once its part was done, no doll would come back for a repeat. For God, we are those dolls, here on the world's stage to play our parts. Once that is done, we are no longer needed. He removes us from the stage. What's all the regret about?

We Indians are supposedly very religious. You only have to say the word 'religion' for the tikis of our holy men to stand straight up. So why are we so afraid of death? Does religion even exist in this country? Ours is a land where you lose your religion by simply touching the wrong person. It's imperative that such a religion be dumped into the Ganga, and good riddance. Human conscience is the biggest religion of all, which we ignore as we immerse ourselves in a tide of sacrilege. Brother kills brother for the sake of a mere cow, or a few insignificant drumbeats. Does that make Bhagwan open the doors of Baikunth to us, or Khoda welcome us into Behast?

It is with great sorrow that I speak thus of a land whose last grain of dust is sacred to me, a land that I must soon leave forever.

We are as well as can be.

Yours affectionately
Chhoto Thakurpo

Alipore Central Jail
Calcutta
June 30, 1931

Ma,

I realize you'll be here at dawn, but I still can't help writing to you.

Your mind must be filled with the lament that God has turned a deaf ear to all your prayers. He must be made of stone, immune to every heartbroken cry of pain. I don't really know what God is, and I can't imagine what He must truly be like, but I do know this much—there's no room for injustice in the world He has created. His justice is a continuing process. Never lose faith in it, try and accept it gladly. How can we possibly know what He intends to do with each action of His?

We fear death, because we give it altogether too much importance. It's exactly the way children fear the bogeyman. Why be so agitated, so disturbed, by the early arrival of that which we know we must all welcome, sooner or later? Must we treat it as the enemy, merely because it announces its coming, instead of turning up unannounced as it usually does?

That's a mistake, you know. Death has appeared to me as nothing less than a friend.

Love and regards from your

Nosu

Alipore Central Jail
Calcutta
June 30, 1931

Dearest brother,

You asked me to write to you, but see, my life has reached its twilight by the time I have had a chance to do so.

What do I say as I leave? All I can say in blessing is, may you be selfless, and may the river of compassion at the pain of others always flow within you.

Brother of mine, do not grieve that I leave you today. Our comings and goings have kept this world alive for eons, and never let its beating heart come to a stop. There's nothing more to say. You will always have all my love and blessings.

Your Dada

For boudi (elder brother's wife), he is the affectionate thakurpo (husband's younger brother). For his younger brother, he is the loving dada (elder brother). For his mother, he is her beloved Nosu.

Dinesh Chandra Gupta.

'Sir, please tell me the story of Khudiram Bose and Prafulla Chaki once more...'

The teacher smiles indulgently at his pupil.

'You heard it only day before yesterday. How many more times...?'

'Just once more...please Sir...'

So begins again the story of Khudiram Bose and Prafulla Chaki's heroic expedition to kill the tyrannical magistrate Kingsford. The pupil listens, unblinking. As he hears how the English tormented the rebels, his face clouds over in anger. At times, he is in tears.

The teacher is particularly fond of this pupil of his. This boy stands apart from the others, a proper daredevil. Even after school is over, he keeps asking for stories about revolutionaries, stories that seem to send him into a trance.

His teacher isn't really surprised. He has heard of the boy's family, and knows that two of his uncles, Dhirendranath and Nagendranath Gupta, were arrested in the Alipore Bomb Case, alongside Aurobindo Ghosh. He understands that rebellion against the Crown flows in his pupil's very blood.

Even as he repeats the story about how Khudiram smiled as he went to his hanging, the teacher wonders if the time has come to induct the boy into the samiti (association). He's young, but possesses in full measure all that is needed to serve the samiti. Pure, undiluted passion for his motherland. And the courage to defy foreign oppression.

'Listen, come around to the samiti tomorrow evening, will you?'

The boy's eyes seem to overflow with joy. He's been desperate to work for the samiti, but unable to ask his teacher for fear of being refused.

Homeward bound, he practically floats on air.

His given name is Sudhir. But almost no one calls him that. They all use his nickname, Badal.

Badal Gupta.

The year is 1928. The Calcutta session of the Indian National Congress has seen the formation of Bengal Volunteers (BV), comprising young men who aspire to free their country. Under the leadership of Major Satya Gupta, and with none other than Subhas Chandra Bose as general officer commanding (GOC), BV grows to become the most active of Bengal's revolutionary associations, with branches in numerous towns, districts and villages.

Its journey is strengthened by the triumvirate of rigorous discipline, practise of gallantry, and a willingness to sacrifice everything for the country. Directly or otherwise, the majority of Bengal's revolutionary leaders are associated with BV.

The list of names is a veritable who's who. 'Master Da' Surjya Sen and Ambika Chakraborty in Chittagong; Surendra Kumar Ghosh in Mymensingh; Madan Mohan Bhowmik in Dhaka; Bipin Behari Ganguly, Bhupendranath Dutta and their comrades in Calcutta; Satin Sen and Manoranjan Gupta in Barisal; Prabhas Chandra Lahiri in Rajshahi and many more.

At the onset of the 1930s, the police's policy of suppressing the rebels through relentless persecution has reached unbearable limits. Random arrests, imprisonment on false charges and inhuman torture in prison have become routine. The top leadership of BV decides that the time has come for a counter-attack, an armed response to the atrocities.

The attack is launched on the morning of 29 August 1930 at Dhaka Medical School and Hospital, where Dhaka's Inspector General (IG) of Police Lowman, accompanied by Superintendent of Police (SP) Hodson are visiting a seriously ill colleague.

As the two senior officers, surrounded by armed guards, walk through the crowds, a student of the medical school moves close to them, unnoticed, and shoots twice, from a distance of fifteen metres. The first bullet is right on target. The infamous Lowman, whose brutality had placed him almost at par with the notorious Charles Tegart, dies on the spot. The second bullet is intended for Hodson, who is hit in the shoulder, and who, as he collapses to the ground, shouts, 'There he is! Get him!'

Benoy, however, knows every inch of the hospital like the back of his hand. The police don't stand a chance, particularly given the large crowds. The twenty-two-year-old becomes a fugitive.

Born in Rohitbhog village of Munshiganj district on 11 September 1908, Benoy Krishna Basu is a student of medicine when he meets the revolutionary Hemchandra Ghosh, and joins a secret outfit called Mukti Sangha. As he becomes an active revolutionary, his career as a medical student comes to an end.

The Raj goes after him with everything it has. He must be caught, this man who has so openly taken the life of the IG. His photo is plastered across the land, at every bus stop, every train station, along every road, in every marketplace, you name it. The police has information that Benoy will try to leave Dhaka for Calcutta. And so every Calcutta-bound train is subject to painstaking searches.

The manner in which Benoy manages to penetrate this apparently impenetrable cover and make his way to Calcutta is hair-raising. His friend Supati Roy is the man who takes on the responsibility of transporting him to Calcutta.

Light-skinned and handsome, aristocratic of bearing, Benoy is disguised as a peasant, in a torn vest and a lungi and a tattered gamchha (cotton towel) around his head. The camouflage is flawless, but unsuitable. There's nothing to be done however. One can only do so much to fake one's real appearance.

Supati himself changes disguises frequently, sometimes as a zamindar's son, and sometimes as a peasant. Dodging the police's searches, the two occasionally take refuge in station waiting rooms, and at other times, Benoy has to feign illness in order to wrap himself from head to toe in a shawl on board a train. By steamer and by train, they make the journey to Dum Dum station. They can't risk getting off at Sealdah because their comrades in Calcutta have sent word that the station premises have been overrun with photographs of Benoy.

Having been entrusted with the task of delivering Benoy safely into the hands of the rebel leadership in Calcutta, Supati performs it flawlessly. At around 10.00 a.m. on 3 September, Benoy and he arrive at 7 Waliullla Lane, to the north of Wellesley Square. The two-storeyed house, a secret shelter, is where revolutionaries Haridas Dutta and Rasamoy Sur have been waiting. Joyfully, they embrace Benoy.

Sudhir 'Badal', Gupta's initiation into the freedom movement happens through BV. Born in East Shimulia village in the Bikrampur region of Dhaka in 1912, he spends his student days at Banaripara High School. Nikunja Sen, his teacher, is intimately associated with the armed freedom struggle and inspires Badal to join BV. This is the man who spends hours telling Badal stories about numerous rebels.

'Sir, please tell me the story of Khudiram Bose and Prafulla Chaki once more...'

Even as an adolescent, Badal demonstrates outstanding organizational skills as he makes his way up the hierarchy. Nikunja and his fellow leaders soon realize that the boy who has not even turned eighteen is ready to take on far bigger responsibilities.

Dinesh Chandra Gupta is ready too. Born in 1911, in Jasholong village of Dhaka, 'Nosu' is the third of eight siblings, four brothers and four sisters. Having taken his matriculation exams in 1926, he is in Midnapore to visit his elder brother Jatish Chandra Gupta. And it is this visit that sows in his mind the dream of setting up a revolutionary association in Midnapore.

The dream is realized two years later, when his single-handed labour results in the formation of the Midnapore chapter of Bengal Volunteers (BV). As an organizer, Dinesh has few equals, and as far as Bengal goes, Midnapore BV is a clear leader, whether in the matter of spreading rural awareness about the revolution or standing up against the injustice of the rulers. Indeed, revolutionaries trained by Dinesh send the local administration into a panic by killing three district magistrates—Douglas, Burge and Peddy—in succession.

Dinesh loves literature with a passion. An ardent admirer

of Rabindranath Tagore, he can effortlessly recite innumerable poems and songs of his from memory.

An excerpt from the memoirs of a contemporary revolutionary records the depth of Dinesh's love for Rabindranath's writings.

'Do you like poetry, Dinesh?

'I do.'

'Why don't you write?'

'Because I love it too much. I've tried a couple of times, actually. Not my job.'

'I know how restless you are, what calms you down?'

'Poetry.'

'The shlokas in the Gita are poetry, too. Why then were you saying the other day that you had to struggle to focus on them?'

'I like reading the Gita, but two lines into it, I start thinking of the battle of Kurukshetra, then about our own battle, and how I want to be a soldier in it! That's the end of my reading.'

'So whose poetry can you calmly focus on?'

'Rabindranath's.'

'Why?'

'I find the wisdom of the Gita in his poems, in my mother tongue, I find this world and all the people in it, I find light and air, animals, green trees…'

'Doesn't his poetry make you more restless?'

'It overwhelms me, but doesn't stir me up. I love it so much that my rushing blood slows down, my mind is captivated. I calm down.'

Literature has to wait, however. Dinesh now has far more important things to do. He and Badal have been summoned to Calcutta, where Benoy is already stationed. The three are instructed to perform an audacious task, so audacious that it will forever haunt the British in their worst nightmares.

Bengal's IG Prisons, Lt Col Norman Simpson, was a man who derived sadistic pleasure from torturing imprisoned rebels. It was his habit to batter with a lathi any inmate jailed on charges of treason. On occasion, he would unleash hardened criminals upon these inmates, and it was on his orders that a bunch of prisoners once brutally assaulted Subhas Chandra Bose in jail. Many of Bose's fellow inmates, men such as Deshapriya Jatindra Mohan, Kiran Shankar Roy and Satya Gupta, also took a beating that day.

Simpson has surrendered his right to live. The monster sahab must be killed, but where? How? Provided the strategy is planned well, he could be killed as he goes about his daily routine, or perhaps at a social gathering. But that will be no different from other such scattered incidents. And merely killing him is not the point. The point is to hit with enough force to shake the British administration to its deepest core, to openly challenge the might of the monarch, to strike at the morale of the ruling dispensation.

The final decision is unprecedented. Simpson must be killed in his own office, in Writers' Building, no less, the heart of the British administration in Bengal, the arrogant embodiment of decades of oppression, standing proud in Dalhousie Square. The revenge drama will be played out in the royal court of the rulers. Let them save Simpson if they can.

Regardless of the mission's success or failure, everyone

knows the chances of getting out alive are next to nothing. Benoy–Badal–Dinesh are doomed to death, or at the very least, to grievous injury. The men themselves, however, feel nothing but an overwhelming delight at the thought of being chosen as Simpson's potential killers. For them, 'life and death merely serve underfoot, and the soul has not a care'.

Only a handful of people are eventually privy to details of the plan. Western outfits are procured, as are firearms along with adequate cartridges. Benoy is transferred from Waliulla Lane to the home of Rajendranath Guha in Metiabruz. Very few knew, even then, that Rajendranath was in any way involved with revolutionaries. Rasamoy would visit Benoy under cover of darkness.

Badal and Dinesh move to a secret location on New Park Street. Supervising them is Nikunja, Badal's Master Moshai.

Operation Simpson is scheduled for 8 December, and it is decided that the trio will meet on Pipe Road, in Khidirpur. Nikunja arrives at the New Park Street house at the appointed time, and is incredulous at the sight that meets his eyes.

Badal and Dinesh, in western clothes, are ready to go. Their journey to death is a mere minutes away, and yet Dinesh, his voice rock steady, is reciting poems by Tagore, as Badal listens, mesmerized.

That brow upon which, fear has not written of slavery
and dust has not etched the mark of shame.
Then, as the long road ends
Life concludes, on weary feet and in blood-soaked garb
I will rise toward the peace that cleanses fatigue
The abode of no sorrow.

Sensing Nikunja's presence, Badal snaps out of his trance.

'Master Moshai, we're ready.'

Dinesh closes his book, and the two friends rise from their chairs. As they check their coat pockets one last time to make sure the revolvers and cartridges are there, Badal slips a phial of potassium cyanide into his pocket. Right, all in order. The journey may begin.

Bharate Shashastra Biplab (Armed Revolution in India), written by Nikunja's friend and comrade-in-arms Bhupendra Kishore Rakshit-Roy, records a significant and detailed description of Dinesh reciting poetry in the moments leading up to the Writers' expedition.

The clock strikes noon as the journey begins. Rasamoy arrives at Pipe Road with Benoy, followed a few minutes later by Nikunja, Badal and Dinesh. The three young men then board a cab, bound for Writers'. Their last ride together.

The rest of the story has been read, reread and discussed ad infinitum. A full history may be found in a contemporary Special Branch file named 'Shooting Outrage in Writers' Building on 8.12.30, Murder of IG Prisons, file number 59/19/30. The narrative that follows below is based on that file, and relevant evidentiary documents. What happened, when and how.

8 December 1930.

As the cab pulls up outside the main gate of Writers' Building, the police officer on duty watches three young men get off, well dressed in European attire. Hat–coat–tie–trousers–boots. Having paid the fare, they stride in confidently, without raising the slightest suspicion in the minds of the officer or his team.

Still confident, they take the stairs to the first floor, where Lt

Col Simpson is in his seat, writing a letter. Next to him stand his personal assistant J.C. Guha and chief peon Bhagal Khan. Outside the door is the assistant peon Fagu Singh.

The long first-floor corridor at Writers' runs west to east. Simpson's office is at the western end, as one turns right from the stairs and walks down the length of the corridor, which looks as it does every day. Impassive orderlies stand outside their sahabs' chambers, and clerks amble past with files and papers under their arms. Visitors wait glumly, not sure when they will be granted an audience with the relevant officials.

Walking briskly, the three young men reach Simpson's room. Fagu Singh eyes them enquiringly.

'Want to see Sahab?'

Benoy answers. 'Yes, is he in?'

'He is, but he's busy. Do you have an appointment? Give me a visiting card if you have one, or write your names in that register. I'll let Sahab know, but you'll have to wait until he can make time for you.'

Wait? No!

As Bhagal Khan emerges from the office, the trio shove both peons aside and push the door open. Their revolvers come out of their coats and into their hands.

Simpson raises his head to find three youths standing in front of his table, their revolvers aimed at him. Terrified, his personal assistant Mr Guha has taken a few steps back. Rooted to the spot, he watches as a hail of bullets tears through Simpson's body. The IG Prisons hasn't had a chance to move, dying as he sits, his end instantaneous.

Jolted back to his senses, Mr Guha emits a fearful cry and runs to the door. Dinesh aims at him, doesn't pull the trigger.

Frantically pushing the door open, Guha runs westwards down the corridor, letting loose ear-splitting cries for help. Fagu Singh rushes to an officer in the next room, named Tufnell-Barrett, who calls Lalbazar, a stone's throw away.

'Shootout here in Writers'! Simpson is shot dead. Armed reinforcement needed at the earliest.'

Commissioner of Police Charles Tegart, realizing that calling for a vehicle will waste precious minutes, decides to simply run to Writers', accompanied by armed members of the Reserve Force. Even at a walk, the distance is covered in two or three minutes. At a run, that comes down to a minute. Tegart and his force get there in no time.

IG Police of Bengal Craig, has emerged from his second-floor office and walked down to the first floor, revolver in hand. Where are the killers who have so effortlessly finished Simpson?

Job done, Benoy–Badal–Dinesh walk down the corridor, west to east, revolvers still drawn. As though on jungle drums, the news has travelled through room after room, and the corridor is deserted, its occupants having sought the nearest shelter they could find. At the mere sight of a curious face peeping out, the three men are opening fire, causing shattered glass windowpanes to cascade to the floor. The otherwise silent corridors reverberate to the cries of 'Bande Mataram', emanating from the valorous trio.

A sergeant called Ford happens to be at Writers' on that day, on personal business and unarmed. He has been standing beside the stairs and watching events unfold. Having descended to the first floor, IG Craig opens fire on the three youths. He misses. Ford grabs the revolver from Craig and fires. And misses.

Benoy–Badal–Dinesh pick up pace. Their chambers are

running out of bullets. They need to reload. When they halt, they find themselves in front of a room belonging to a senior officer called Nelson. Right next door is the passport office, which Benoy and Badal enter in order to load their revolvers. The few occupants rush out in terror.

Dinesh, who has remained outside Nelson's office, is reloading swiftly, when Nelson himself pushes the door open and peers out. Dinesh fires instantly, hitting Nelson in the thigh, and chases him back into the room. Though wounded, the robustly built Nelson now begins to wrestle with Dinesh, trying to snatch his revolver. Hearing the shot, Benoy and Badal come out of the passport office, revolvers loaded. Benoy whips Nelson across the head with the butt of his revolver, knocking him to the floor, from where he manages to stagger out, bleeding heavily. Meanwhile, the three men run back into the passport office.

Between 12.30 and 12.45 p.m., when the three young sons of Bengal held sway over the corridors, the police have literally been rooted to the spot. Until the Reserve Force arrives from Lalbazar, and takes positions, not a single soul other than IG Craig and Sergeant Ford has shown the nerve to confront the intruders. This, despite the fact that the second floor accommodates several high-ranking police officers, and there is more than one staircase to the floor below.

Things change with the arrival of reinforcements. The passport office in which Benoy–Badal–Dinesh are closeted is effectively surrounded. Opening the door a crack, Dinesh lets off two rounds through it, but the police are alert and the shots fly wide. An officer called Jones returns fire, and there is a cry of pain from Dinesh. A bullet has probably found his shoulder.

The young trio are trapped. Outside, armed policemen are posted on both sides of the door. The long corridor is also under the control of men in uniform. The three exchange looks—they have known all along that, short of a miracle, they were never going to get out of this alive. Now, with capture imminent, and bullets running out, they prepare themselves for death.

Taking the potassium cyanide from his pocket, Badal empties the entire phial down his throat. In about a minute, his lifeless body slumps down on the table. The policemen standing outside now hear two successive shots from the room. Both Benoy and Dinesh have shot themselves in the head.

Looking in through a gap at the bottom of a door on the eastern side, Deputy Commissioner Bartley spots two bodies on the ground, the floor awash in blood. The police finally push the door open.

Next to Dinesh lies a .455 bore Webley revolver, with two cartridge shells in the chamber, one fired, the other misfired. The back pocket of Benoy's trousers produces a five-chamber .34 bore Ivor Johnson revolver. And near Badal's body lie two .32 bore six-chamber American revolvers, a few cartridges and the empty phial of potassium cyanide.

Scattered around the floor are a fairly large number of shells, and three foreign-made hats. Two flags of the Indian National Congress lie unheeded in the dust, and one more is in the back pocket of Benoy's trousers. The Writers' corridor yields roughly twenty bullet heads.

Badal's body is sent off to the mortuary, while a police vehicle rushes Benoy and Dinesh to Medical College Hospital. The Lalbazar top brass knows exactly how important it is that the two are kept alive, and grilled for information once they are well enough.

The next day, front pages of newspapers across the country are devoted to the incident, which has shaken not just Bengal, but the whole of India. Here's what the 9 December edition of *Anandabazar Patrika* has to say:

Tuesday, December 9, 1930

Bengal's Inspector General of Prisons Shot Dead

Yesterday at noon, an extraordinary and daring murder was committed in the heart of Calcutta, at Writers' Building, where three young Bengali men shot and killed Bengal's Inspector General of Prisons, Lt. Col. Simpson.

The three young Bengali men appeared in the office of the Inspector General of Prisons between 12.30 and 12.45 p.m. Col. Simpson was inside his office, talking to his personal assistant. When the three youths expressed a desire to meet him, the peon asked them to wait since Col. Simpson was busy, and asked them to state the purpose of their visit on a piece of paper, as is customary. The young men, however, refused to do so and, pushing him aside, entered the room, rapidly firing at Col. Simpson 5-6 times, instantly causing his death.

Leaving the room, the assailants moved down the corridor. As they ran, they kept firing at the glass windows and ceilings of the various offices. Finance Secretary Mr Marr's office windows bear bullet marks, as does the office of Mr J.W. Nelson.

Next, they entered the passport office and shot at an American, but the bullet missed him. No peon was hit.

The assailants then went into Mr Nelson's room and shot him in the thigh. However, his injury is not serious.

News Update

According to the latest update, one of the assailants has taken his own life, while the other two are in critical condition. One of them has been identified as Benoy Krishna Basu, who has apparently issued a dying statement, stating that he is indeed Benoy Krishna Basu, and he is the killer of Mr Lowman.

All three assailants were dressed in the manner of Europeans, and raised a cry of 'Bande Mataram' as they moved along the corridor, firing all the while…

Doctors try everything within their power, but Benoy is beyond saving, and draws his last breath on 13 December, a martyr forever. Two days before his death, his father appeals to the British government to allow him to see his son for the last time. By now, he knows Benoy will never come back to him. The government grants his request.

Everyone's attention is now focused on keeping Dinesh alive. Miraculously, he does make it back from death's door. And the trial for the case begins under a Special Tribunal headed by Sessions Judge Ralph Reynolds Garlick. It is, however, a trial in name only. A death sentence is the only possible conclusion to the farcical proceedings.

Concluding his verdict, Justice Garlick writes, 'The punishment of murder is death. We are asked to refrain from passing the death sentence on the ground that the case is not free from doubt. But though there is some doubt about particular incidents of the story, we have no doubt at all that Dinesh was one of the three men who murdered Col Simpson… We unanimously find Dinesh Chandra Gupta guilty of murder and sentence him under Sec 302 IPC to be hanged by the neck until he is dead.'

At 4.45 a.m. in Alipore Jail on 7 July 1931, the nineteen-year-old Dinesh wears a noose around his neck, but celebrates life, his powerful, resonant voice calling 'Bande Mataram!' as he makes the journey from his cell to the hanging area.

The order for Dinesh's death adds to the resentment among Bengal's rebel units. Numerous public signature campaigns requesting that the hanging be stalled find their way to the governor only to be rejected.

In their desperate bid to prevent a breakdown of law and order, the authorities try and keep the date and time of Dinesh's hanging a secret. The bid fails. The next morning, Deshapriya Jatindra Mohan Sengupta's newspaper, *Advance,* runs the headline, 'Dauntless Dinesh Dies at Dawn!'

The 7 July edition of *Anandabazar Patrika* reports, 'Dinesh Gupta was hanged in the last hours of Monday. On Tuesday morning, every street crossing of the city saw a strong police presence. This makes it fairly certain that the hanging is done.'

Ralph Reynolds Garlick, the moving force behind Dinesh's death sentence, met his own end soon enough. On 27 July, a mere twenty days after Dinesh's hanging, Garlick was shot and killed in his busy courtroom by Kanailal Bhattacharya, the rebel hero from Joynagar, whose story is also to be found in this book.

During his imprisonment, Dinesh wrote several letters to his family. Those letters stand witness to a nineteen-year-old's deeply philosophical approach to life, the incredible breadth of his vision.

On the one hand, he wrote to his sister-in-law, 'Ours is a land where you lose your religion by simply touching the wrong person. It's imperative that such a religion be dumped into the Ganga, and good riddance.'

On the other hand, he offered a life lesson to his younger brother, 'Our comings and goings have kept this world alive for eons, and never let its beating heart come to a stop.'

In the same breath, he consoled his devastated mother, 'His justice is a continuing process. Never lose faith in it, try and accept it gladly.'

On the eve of the hanging, he wrote to his mother again.

Alipore Central Jail
Calcutta
5.00 p.m.
6 July 1931

Ma,

I will not see you again. But I wait for you in the world beyond this.

I have never been able to do much for you. No one will know, and I don't want anyone to know, how deeply my inability has hurt me.

Please, forgive me all my faults, all my sins.

Love and regards from your

Nosu

Benoy–Badal–Dinesh. The men whose names established a new identity for Kolkata's Dalhousie Square, post-Independence, and whose epic Writers' expedition will forever enrich the annals of history.

Benoy Krishna Basu, born 1908
Dinesh Chandra Gupta, born 1911
Sudhir 'Badal' Gupta, born 1912

Tradition dictates that we mention the year of passing for those no longer with us. There's no need in this case. For they are the deathless. What does physical cessation matter, when the assurance of immortality transcends the boundaries of date, space and self?

Sudhir 'Badal' Gupta

Benoy Krishna Basu

Dinesh Chandra Gupta

Statues of the trio

Nikunja Sen

Supati Roy

Chapter 9

REVENGE WILL BE MINE: KANAILAL BHATTACHARYA

IT ISN'T A forest, really, just a fairly large plot of land covered by trees and thick undergrowth, a mere seven minutes from Topsia on foot. The breaking dawn still carries the aroma of the night, and the nineteen-year-old takes it all in. This isn't his first time in Calcutta, but this place is completely unfamiliar. Without being told, nobody will ever guess it is inside the city—so green, so quiet. And why has Sunil Da brought him here at the crack of dawn?

'I'm about to test you today...let's see if you pass...see that tree?'

Quite an impressive tree it is, as wide as it is tall—almost invokes respect, and a second, more detailed, look. Sunil walks straight to the tree and, taking a bit of chalk out of his pocket, draws a circle on the massive trunk.

'Here it is, your shooting range. There are six bullets in the chamber, which means all you have are six chances. Move back...a little farther...yes...perfect.'

Sunil hands the revolver to the young man, patting him lightly on the back. As the youth takes position, all kinds of thoughts rush through his mind, his nerves tingling. *So this is going to be target practice? Why hadn't Sunil Da said so? At least there would have been time for some mental preparation. Hardly fair to spring it on one so suddenly.*

Or perhaps the secrecy has been deliberate? Does he just want to see how quickly I can prepare myself mentally? If that is the case, he must be thinking of giving me something to do. The young man feels excitement coursing through his veins, and silently reprimands himself...overeagerness will make him miss the target...he needs to focus. Standing at the specified distance, he takes aim—the chalk circle his bull's eye.

Sunil stands behind him, smoking. And watching.

Two of the six are misses. Four hit the target, bang in the middle of the circle. Sunil walks to the trunk and looks carefully at the result. Then he walks quietly back, and envelops the young man in a hug. 'Well done!'

'Does this mean I'm ready for action? Sunil Da?'

Sunil smiles as he places a hand on his back. 'Hold on, why so impatient?'

The arrangements are enough to put any grand wedding preparations to shame. Young men and students throng the venue, even this early in the morning. The office of the samiti (association) is being draped in tricolour flags. But the modest room is evidently not big enough for the eventual turnout. Word has spread, and young men are expected to arrive in droves from surrounding villages. The only solution is to set up a platform out in the open. And so work has duly begun, with wooden planks being assembled, and tables and chairs draped in white being put up.

Senior members of the samiti dash around, looking exactly like the harried father of a bride. Where's the microphone, has it come yet? Weren't there supposed to be of flag garlands on the street? I can't see a single one! You mean to say nobody has had time to sweep the room? Hurry up, please, all of you. He'll be here in just about two hours!

'He' is the chief guest at the annual gathering of the Joynagar Byayam Samiti (roughly, Joynagar Fitness Association). 'His' impending presence has caused a tidal wave of enthusiasm in the entire area, and limited means have posed no hurdle to the elaborate preparations.

As the car enters the narrow lane where the association is located, the surrounding area is a sea of dark heads, the cheering and chanting constant. The serene, tall man emerges from the car, and climbs emphatically to the dais. At the very outset, he calls out, 'Bande Mataram!'

Netaji Subhas Chandra Bose! The waiting crowd explodes with joy at the sight of his familiar face, and a thousand voices roar, 'Bande Mataram!'

Byayam Samiti Chief Sunil Chatterjee is struck by the cheering young man in the very first row of the crowd. Bright of eye and sturdy of build, he raises his fist in the air as he belts out slogans, the veins in his neck standing out. Who is the boy? His face seems familiar, so he must be a local, but Sunil has never seen him at the samiti. Looks exactly like the kind of youth they need. He'll find out more once Netaji leaves. Who *is* the boy?

'Ma, I'm leaving Calcutta for a few days, could be longer.'

'Where are you going? What do you mean longer? How much longer? What are you up to? And who's going with you?'

His impatience at his mother's questions is obvious.

'I can't tell you how much longer. It's a job for the samiti.'

The middle-aged woman sighs, but says nothing more. Over the past several days, she has accepted the fact that no matter how many times she asks, she will receive no answers, now that her son has found this brand new passion, the samiti.

It has been desperately difficult to make ends meet ever since her husband's death. Her elder son has a decent job in Calcutta, but she is endlessly troubled by her younger son. Never one for books and studies, now that he has turned nineteen he needs to find some sort of occupation, surely? But no, all his days and nights seem to be devoted to the blessed samiti. She has heard the neighbours talk. The samiti is a fitness association in name only. What is really is, is a hub of anti-British activities.

Her fears have deepened ever since. Her son has always been a daredevil—what kind of trouble is he inviting by associating with those swadeshis? Just look at him...won't even tell her how long he will be away, nor where he's going, or why. Is it any wonder she's afraid? Not that he cares, of course.

'Stop worrying, will you, Ma? I've told you I'll write if it takes too long.'

'Lt Col Simpson was shot dead. Mr J.W. Nelson, judicial secretary, was wounded in the leg. Another bullet narrowly missed Mr A. Marr, Finance member...'

Thus reads an excerpt from a report in *The Statesman*, dated 9 December 1930. The subject is the hair-raising and audacious assault on Writers' Building by Benoy–Badal–Dinesh, culminating in the 'Battle of the Corridors', on 8 December. As the world knows, Badal takes potassium cyanide after Simpson's killing, his death almost instant. Benoy shoots himself in the head, breathing his last at the Medical College Hospital on 13 December. Dinesh Gupta is the sole survivor, despite a self-inflicted gunshot to the head and a large dose of poison.

Nobody can accuse the British government of neglecting Dinesh's treatment. Indeed, he is given every possible care so that the fearless soldier can be prepared for the farce known as a Special Tribunal trial, which sentences him to death, intending to send a message to his fellow armed revolutionaries. As 7 July 1931 dawns, Dinesh embarks on his final journey, a trapdoor opening up beneath his feet, a noose around his neck.

A newspaper headline reads, 'Dauntless Dinesh Dies at Dawn.' The Calcutta Corporation passes a resolution that says, 'This Corporation records its sense of grief at the execution of Dinesh Chandra Gupta who sacrificed his life in the pursuit of his ideal.'

Dinesh's hanging proves to be the spark that lights the suppressed fury among Bengal's revolutionaries. Members of Bengal Volunteers (BV), a branch of which Dinesh himself had founded in Midnapore, explode in anger, the idea of swift retaliatory action taking shape almost immediately. And the first victim becomes District Magistrate Col James Peddy, killed by Jotijibon Ghosh and Bimal Dasgupta. The latter is declared a marked man by the police, but vanishes without a trace.

The killing of Peddy, however, is more a spontaneous act

of revenge. The principal target is Special Tribunal president Ralph Reynolds Garlick, the man who ordered the hanging of Dinesh. The man who is forever on the warpath against undertrial revolutionaries, harsh beyond reason on anyone accused of rebellion against the government.

So Garlick deserves to be repaid, is the decision. But who will do the job?

Kanailal Bhattacharya. An energetic nineteen-year-old resident of Majilpur, under Joynagar police station. This is the young man who has attracted the attention of revolutionary leader Sunil Chatterjee at the annual meeting of the Joynagar Byayam Samiti, with his enthusiastic cheering for Netaji. But who *is* he, really? Sunil intends to find out once the meeting is over. 'Sat Da' needs to be informed, as well.

Sat Da, a.k.a. Satkari Bandopadhyay, is a homoeopathic physician with a demanding practice in Baruipur. Along with his patients, though, his chamber is also full of groups of young men, members of several revolutionary outfits in 24 Parganas, for whom he is a father figure. Sat Da himself trusts Sunil completely, and the founding of the Joynagar–Majilpur samiti has his unspoken blessing. Netaji is particularly fond of Dr Satkari, and it is at the latter's request that Netaji agreed to visit the samiti, to boost the morale of the revolutionaries.

As the mission to kill Garlick progresses, Sat Da entrusts Sunil with the responsibility of finding a suitable boy. The instructions are clear: while on the assignment, the assassin will not only carry a revolver, but also poison. If he can escape once the deed is done, well and good; if not, it has to be suicide. Capture and arrest are simply not on the list of options.

Finding the 'boy' hasn't proved difficult for Sunil. By now, Kanai has joined the samiti, his initiation into the revolutionary ideal complete. A bunch of young Turks in the samiti is desperate for action. Forget ideological discussions and long-term plans, their prime assets are passion and valour. They need to do something for their country, and if they die doing it, fair enough.

Kanai stands out in this crowd. Inherently well-built, he doesn't need the exercise room at the samiti. All he does, every evening, is to pursue Sunil doggedly.

'Aren't you going to give me an assignment? I don't like all this wrestling and stick fighting any more. Please give me a chance, now that I've learnt how to shoot.'

As July 1931 draws to a close, Kanai's 'chance' materializes. Sunil has a rented second-floor room in a Hazra Road mess, where he stays whenever he comes to Calcutta, and it has been the venue for several secret revolutionary meetings. The room remains locked otherwise, and Sunil now instructs two of his associates to bring Kanai to Calcutta from Joynagar.

On 25 July, Kanai is startled by the sudden summons, but a little excited as well. Coincidentally, his mother is in Calcutta too, staying with her elder son. As soon as he reaches the mess, Kanai bombards Sunil with questions, but all he receives in response are a smile and a mild pat on the back.

'You'll know when the time comes. Just wake up early tomorrow, I'll take you somewhere.'

'Somewhere' is the overgrown piece of land near Topsia, where Sunil hands the revolver to Kanai and tests his skills.

'This is your shooting range, there are six bullets in the chamber. Which means just six chances...'

By now, Kanai has a good idea of the 'action' he has been selected for. Sunil is still being fairly secretive, and has brought him to Alipore Court after lunch, apparently to show him around the place. 'This is the munsif court, where the sub-judges sit. The large room is the bar library. And this elongated area here is where the typists sit. Mark our entry and exit points carefully. Come on, before we leave, I'll show you the courtroom of the sessions judge on the first floor, where Garlick sits.'

Garlick! Kanai feels an instant surge of adrenaline. The same Garlick who had ordered the hanging of Dinesh Gupta? Impulsively, Kanai grabs Sunil's hand.

'Sunil Da! So is it...'

Sunil firmly reins him in.

'Haven't I told you to be patient? Keep calm and study the room.'

A sergeant armed with a revolver stands guard in front of the room. Garlick has been receiving several death threats of late, and the government has strengthened his security detail within the courtroom. The sergeant's keen eye measures everyone entering the room, whether lawyer or ordinary visitor. Entering the courtroom, Sunil takes a seat on a bench. Next to him, Kanai coolly examines the room, absorbing every detail. A few burly men stand behind the judge. Plainclothesmen?

As they make their way back from the court, through a monsoon downpour, Sunil buys a pair of canvas shoes for Kanai, who is carrying the umbrella he brought from Joynagar. By the time they return to the mess, twilight has won over the late afternoon.

'Kanai...do something...go see your mother quickly. Isn't she staying with your brother?'

'Yes...'

'Tell her...you're going out of Calcutta on work...you may be late coming back.'

As Kanai's mother serves him dinner that night, he ignores her anxious questions.

'Stop worrying, will you, Ma? I've told you I'll write if it takes too long.'

Once he's back in the mess, Kanai learns about the whole plan from Sunil. His guess has proved correct. Garlick is to be killed as revenge for Dinesh's hanging. Sunil hands Kanai paper and pen.

'Here...write...'

'What?'

'Write ... "Bande Mataram! May you be destroyed; here's your reward for the unlawful hanging of Dinesh Gupta; Regards, Bimal Gupta".'

'Done...now what?'

'Keep this note in your right pocket and this phial of potassium cyanide in your left. The six-chamber revolver goes inside your umbrella. Careful, it's loaded. The Suicide Squad list with the police has no mention of any Kanailal Bhattacharya. Nobody knows you. That's an advantage. God forbid, if you can't escape, take the poison. When they find the note in your pocket, the police will assume you're Bimal Dasgupta, the man who vanished after killing Magistrate Peddy. They'll realize their mistake later, but they won't trace the real killer any time soon. Got it?'

Kanai nods, and Sunil continues.

'You will leave first, around noon. I'll follow a little later in a taxi. I'll go upstairs to check on you, and come back to the taxi. I'll have to put some make-up on you, too, tomorrow.'

27 July 1931. Kanai is in full battle gear. In other words, he looks exactly like a harmless country bumpkin, with his tousled hair, and his pleated dhoti riding up to his knees. He has on a dirty shirt, buttoned all the way to the neck, and a coat, his new canvas shoes on his feet. The umbrella in his hand hides a loaded .380 bore firearm. At around noon, he hops on to an Alipore-bound tram.

An hour later, the taxi carrying Sunil comes to a halt under the sessions court porch. The driver, Prem Singh, is an old acquaintance of Sunil's. He knows these men are fighting the British, and are mixed up in all kinds of danger. He never displays any overt curiosity, but is always at their beck and call, day or night. Today, for instance, all it took was a single summons from Sunil for him to drop everything else and come right away.

Sunil goes upstairs, to find that Garlick is out to lunch, but expected to return soon. Kanai is seated meekly among the waiting courtroom crowd. His disguise is so flawless that it has not aroused a single suspicion in the mind of the sharp-eyed sergeant standing in the doorway. Sunil comes back down, and gets into the taxi.

'Singh Ji...keep the engine running...drive as soon as I say so.'

At exactly 2.00 p.m., Garlick is back in his courtroom. Everyone rises respectfully. Garlick sits, and the hearing begins.

'Milord...my humble submission before the learned court is that...'

As Garlick attentively makes notes while listening to the lawyer, his head bent, Kanai decides the time has come. Rising to his feet, he can scarcely believe his good fortune. This man has taken the life of Dinesh Gupta, condemned so many more to prison...the opportunity to kill him is almost a sacred one, not available to many.

Before anyone realizes what is happening, Kanai has reached the vacant witness box in one fluid movement. The room isn't very large, and the distance between the box and the judge's table isn't too great. The first bullet flies to the ceiling...even before an alarmed Garlick can properly respond to the shot, Kanai has leapt on to the handrail around the witness box. Another leap, much shorter than the ones he routinely practises at the samiti, and he is on Garlick's table. At nearly point-blank range, he fires straight at the judge's forehead. Two bullets, in succession. Bull's eye. Garlick felled in his own courtroom.

Stunned by the unexpected sequence of events, the plainclothesmen finally open fire. And miss. Kanai's counterfire catches one of them in the shoulder. The noise has brought the sergeant running into the room, firing at Kanai. Two shots find his stomach and leg, and a few more rounds are pumped into his fallen body. Taking no chances, Kanai has by then emptied the entire contents of the phial of potassium cyanide into his mouth. And there's a second death in the courtroom.

Pandemonium reigns as the room's terrified occupants rush out. The exodus has upset tables, chairs, benches. Papers are strewn all over the place. A call has gone out to Lalbazar from the adjoining room, pleading for armed units. An ambulance has been summoned from the hospital.

Outside the court, Sunil sits absolutely still in the taxi, smoking constantly. Is it done? Why isn't Kanai back? He doesn't know then that the man he is waiting for is lying lifeless in the courtroom. Watching the commotion as people run helter-skelter, he asks a lawyer, 'What's wrong?'

The reply is immediate.

'Garlick shot dead. Assailant dead too!'

Sunil listens, and says no more. 'Singh Ji, start the car,' he calmly tells the driver.

Here's an exact transcription of the police report of the incident:

> On 27th July 1931 at 2 p. m., Mr R.R. Garlick, I.C.S., Senior Sessions Judge, 24 Parganas, was while sitting in Court, fatally shot through the head by a Bengali Youth.
>
> The assassin, who was immediately shot down by the Sergeant on duty, committed suicide while lying wounded under the table, by swallowing cyanide of potassium from a phial which was found on the floor. The Police Surgeon, who held the postmortem examination, was of the opinion that death was due to hydro-cyanic acid poisoning. A bullet of .450 bore, which was extracted from the body, was evidently that fired from the revolver of the Sergeant. In the left hip pocket of the deceased was found a slip of paper with a bullet hole through it, on which was written 'Bande Mataram; Cursed be your Court, whose injustice condemned Dinesh Gupta to

> execution. Receive the reward for it.—Bimal Gupta'; while in the other pocket were found 14 live revolver cartridges of .380 bore.
>
> The revolver which was found in the possession of the assailant is a 6-chambered .380 bore, with fall out cylinder, marked 'Jupitre' with trademark 'E.C.' and bearing the number 15621 on the heel of the butt and also the word 'Eiber'. It bears Spanish proof mark and the cylinder rotates from right to left. The four live cartridges in the revolver and the fourteen live cartridges found in the coat pocket of the assassin bear the base mark 'S. & W. .38 Spl.' and each charged with 16 grs. black powder and weighing 140 grs.
>
> The photograph of the deceased assassin was definitely identified by a deponent on 29th October 1932 as that of one Kanai Lal Bhattacharji, son of Nagendra Nath, of Majilpur police station Joynagar, 24-Parganas. Mr Garlick was the President of the Special Tribunal which on 2nd February 1931 convicted and sentenced to death Dinesh Ch. Gupta for the murder of Lt. Col. N. Simpson, IMS Inspector-General of Prisons, Bengal, at Writers' Buildings, Calcutta, on 8th December 1930. Sunil Chatarji's group of the Juganta Party was responsible for this outrage. (File 439/31)

Senior Lalbazar officials rush to the spot and recover the piece of paper from Kanai's pocket...'May you be destroyed' ... Who is this Bimal Gupta? The untraced killer of Peddy, Bimal Dasgupta? The police gets in touch with Dasgupta's family, and discover very soon that this isn't him. So who is he?

Lalbazar left no stone unturned in their attempts to identify 'him'. A last-ditch, desperate effort was made in the form of a newspaper advertisement: 'A reward is hereby declared, worth

Rupees Five Hundred, to be given to one who can identify the murderer of Mr Garlick.'

No one came forward. A year and three months after the courtroom incident, someone identified Kanai from a photograph of his corpse. The rebels had won. Garlick killed, and the police clueless about the conspiracy behind it. What could they do? It had taken them so long to simply identify the assailant.

Kanai had told his mother he would write if he was away for too long. She had waited and waited for a letter. It never came. The bad news did.

Kanai was just one of them—the nameless. Those who didn't think twice before putting their lives on the line, laughing in the face of death. They had no expectations of immortality, no secret desire to find a place in history. History returned the favour by steadfastly refusing to record the honour due to them. Inevitably, oblivion has taken over.

We forgot, we forget.

Kanailal Bhattacharya

Courtroom

Ralph Reynolds Garlick

Bimal Dasgupta

Satkari Bandopadhyay

Registered No. C603
For official use only.

No. 588

Bengal Criminal Intelligence Gazette

Illustrated Supplement

[To be detached and filed with other Illustrated Supplements]

For permanent record

Property of the Government of Bengal

Published by Authority

CALCUTTA, FRIDAY, SEPTEMBER 4, 1931.

Reward, Rs. 500.

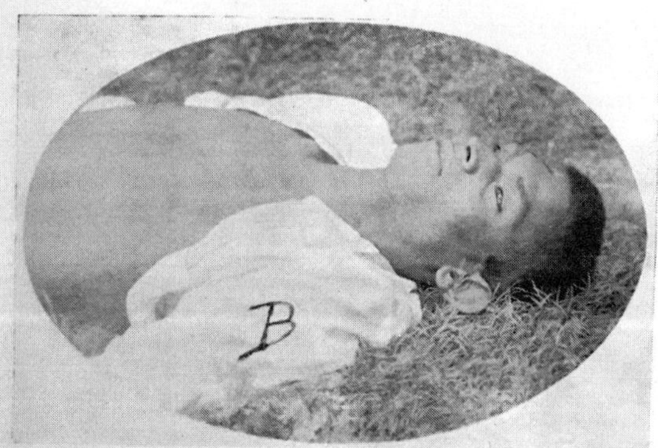

I. B., C. I. D., Bengal (Murderer, an unknown—Reward for identification of).—In continuation of Illustrated Supplement No. 586 to the Bengal C. I. Gazette, dated 31-7-1931,

Bengal Criminal Intelligence Gazette declaring reward for identification of the body of the assassin of Ralph Reynolds Garlick

Chapter 10

THE GALLANT GIRL: BINA DAS

THE FIRST TIME.

She's seen photographs, never the real thing. Picking up the metallic firearm, the young woman looks at it from every angle, turning it around in her hands, thrill and excitement rushing through her veins. So *this* is a revolver, a real live one! But what about bullets, cartridges? Unable to stop herself, she blurts out the question.

'Didi...bullet?'

Sensing her restlessness, Didi smiles fondly.

'Later. First, I need to show you how to use this thing. This is a tool that will not obey you unless you understand it. Give it to me...'

Reluctantly, the young woman hands over the revolver. And Didi begins her explanation.

'You wanted bullets? This is where the bullets go...the chamber. Open it, like this, and insert the bullets one by one into these five holes. Watch how I close the chamber. Done? That's it. Your revolver is now loaded.'

The young woman listens with rapt attention.

'This is the barrel, from where the bullet will emerge once you press the trigger. Remember, always; when you're loading...I mean putting bullets into the chamber, the barrel must never face you, ever. If, by any chance, you press the trigger, that's the end of you. Always load it sideways, like this.

'But the important thing about shooting is grip, how you're holding the weapon. Watch how I hold it, where my fingers are. Try? Now, aim. This thing you see rising from the front end of the barrel is called the "foresight U". If you can keep this in a straight line with the target, you have fewer chances of missing. Let's say I'm shooting you in the head…move back a little…watch…how I align the foresight U in a straight line with your head…

'When you shoot, don't press the trigger with all your strength, a slight pressure is enough. And yes, most important, make sure your arm is dead straight, from shoulder to wrist. It should be locked, almost no muscle movement. Got all of it? It will become easier after a few days of dry practice, without bullets. And now, here you go.'

So saying, the woman extracts a small leather pouch from her shoulder bag, and upturns it onto the table. With a clinking sound, a dozen cartridges roll out. The younger woman begins practising the loading process. One…two…three…four…

Didi watches intently, and then asks, her voice quiet, 'You can do it, can't you?'

The young woman lifts her eyes, her cheerful smile replaced with grim determination. Didi now takes yet another packet out of her bag.

'Keep this.'

'What is it?'

'Potassium cyanide.'

What's going on here today? Some big gun's visit? Why so many policemen?

The College Street neighbourhood has been the scene of hectic activity all morning. On normal days, as the day progresses, the patrol vehicle from Jorasanko police station makes the occasional appearance. The picture is very different today. Several police vehicles have been criss-crossing the area since early morning. There are armed police personnel at every street corner, guns very obviously on display. Well-built plainclothesmen roam the area, alert. Even at a glance, it is clear that they are policemen, not ordinary pedestrians. Senior officers from Lalbazar are making frequent rounds too, to supervise the arrangements.

So what's going on here today? Who's visiting?

The governor himself, that's who. His Excellency the Governor of Bengal Sir Stanley Jackson, chief guest at the University of Calcutta's annual convocation ceremony, to be held in the Senate Hall, will hand over certificates to the students. The ceremony will also host several other important guests, and Calcutta Police is not prepared to risk the slightest security breach. The cordon around the university is seamless, not even a fly can slip in.

One after another, cars enter College Street and stop at the university entrance. The guests walk in, so do the cheerfully noisy students. They're dressed differently today, the traditional black gowns of a convocation covering their everyday attire of dhotis or trousers or saris. It's their day, and they light up the place.

Gasping for breath, her voice quivering in agitation, Ila Sen, a student of Bethune College, reaches her college gates.

'Just heard…the police are about to beat up the Presidency picketers to get them to move. A force has left Lalbazar. They may even shoot.'

'What? Let's go!'

The group of girl students from Bethune and other colleges, staging a picket in front of Bethune College in support of the Civil Disobedience programme, set off en masse for Presidency College on College Street, the city's 'book zone', which is by now reverberating to the students' cries of 'Bande Mataram!'

When the girls arrive, College Street has become a war zone, end to end, and the police are involved in a fierce tussle with the Presidency students. Under no circumstances will the men in uniform allow the picketing to continue, and the students are equally determined that it shall. Traffic comes to a complete standstill as the thoroughfare shuts down.

The lathi charge having proved more or less ineffective, the officer-in-charge of the force orders the armed guards to get ready to fire.

In an instant, the girls make up their minds. Shoot, will they? Bring it on, then. Let's see how many bullets they have. Hand in hand, the girls form a barricade in front of the Presidency boys. If they shoot, they'll have to shoot us first.

It is a sight to behold. The human chain formed by the girls encircles the agitating Presidency students. This is war, and not an inch of ground will be ceded. As the police stand confounded, taken aback by this militant stand, the guns lose their shine.

The officer restrains his men. It is out of the question to shoot at a group of unarmed college girls. The heat from that particular fire will scorch not just Bengal, but the entire nation. Unable to risk it, the police back down. Back to Lalbazar.

About to leave, the officer casts a last, admiring glance at the young woman standing right in the centre of the human chain. The young woman who, moments earlier, has looked him straight in the eye and announced calmly, in flawless English, 'Break the cordon if you must…but be sure, over our dead bodies.'

Who is the girl? She doesn't look to be more than eighteen or nineteen, at most. Where does such courage come from at this age?

Lost in thought, the officer starts the car, the cheers from the girls ringing in his ears. 'Bande Mataram!' And he hears, sung in chorus, snatches of a song by Rabindranath Tagore, 'Fear not, for you shall conquer, the doors will open…'

Beni Madhab Das is the headmaster of Cuttack's Ravenshaw Collegiate School, his family made up of wife Sarala and daughters Kalyani and Bina. This is the same Beni Madhab whom the British government had charged with spreading treason in school, causing his overnight transfer to Krishnanagar. He is the same legendary teacher whose nationalistic ideals created a deep impact on the consciousness of one of his students in Cuttack, a boy called Subhas Chandra Bose.

Apart from their parents, Kalyani and Bina were also deeply influenced by their maternal uncle, Professor Binayendra Nath Sen, founder of Neeti Vidyalaya, whose impact on building the character of a nation proved far-reaching.

In the evenings, Beni Madhab would tell his daughters stories about venerable social revolutionaries from across the world, and their sacrifices for their nations. The two girls would listen, entranced.

Sarala would break in. 'Aren't you two going to bed? It's very late, and you have school tomorrow!'

'Ma...just a little bit more, please...let Baba finish this story.'

Smiling indulgently, Sarala would think, this was actually what the girls should be listening to, it would build character. And she would join her husband and daughters in the storytelling session.

Sarala possessed rare organizational abilities, having single-handedly set up Punyashram for destitute women, alongside actively participating in the running of Neeti Vidyalaya established by her brother.

Kalyani was born in 1907, and Bina in 1911. Growing up in the early twentieth century, against the backdrop of the nationwide movement for freedom, under the influence of liberal-minded, educated parents, it was natural that the two youngsters would step beyond the confines of a mundane, traditional upbringing and begin to feel the pain of a colonized nation.

Having inherited her mother's organizational skills, Kalyani, who comes to Calcutta to study for her postgraduate degree in 1928, helps establish Chhatri Sangha (roughly, Girl Students' Association), alongside classmates Surama Mitra, Kamala Dasgupta and others, with Surama as president and Kalyani as secretary. Starting out as an association of girl students of Calcutta's schools and colleges, the organization gradually expands to include students like Pritilata Waddedar, Kalpana Dutta, Suhasini Ganguly and Sulata Kar, who would later become active participants in the freedom struggle. Also joining the organization is Bina, then a student of St John's Diocesan Girls' Higher Secondary School on Elgin Road.

The members of Chhatri Sangha spend their days in hectic activity. Once classes are over for the day, they either train in stick fighting under Dinesh Majumdar, a member of the revolutionary society Jugantar, or spend long hours practising how to use a knife, or jump into the College Square swimming pool, or sharpen their bicycling skills. Alongside there are lessons on basic first aid.

With the country up in arms against its British rulers, how can Chhatri Sangha escape the heat of battle? The students are resolute about keeping themselves mentally and physically fit for any eventuality, prepared to make any sacrifice for the good of the nation.

The Civil Disobedience movement, making waves across the country, finds allies in college after college in Calcutta, where pickets become a regular feature, and campuses echo to the cries of 'Bande Mataram'. In particular, the prolonged and vociferous picket staged by students of Presidency College causes some concern in Lalbazar.

Stern repression is the only way, is the conclusion. A force sets off for College Street, with clear instructions to shoot if necessary, should a beating not be enough. We have already seen what happens next—the arrival of the Bethune College girls, the human chain and a disconcerted police force abandoning the battle for the time being.

Who is the girl who leads the fight back, who so impresses the hardened officer from Lalbazar? A girl who can stare down the barrel of a gun and announce, 'over our dead bodies'.

Her name is Bina Das. Unlike her calm, organized sister Kalyani, Bina is emotional, a little reckless, even. Hugely popular in school among both friends and teachers for her sweet nature, she is both academically brilliant and unparalleled when it comes to debating, public speaking or story writing. Her teachers have high hopes for her future. They know that whatever she chooses to do, whether she joins the Indian Civil Service or becomes a teacher, she will be a roaring success.

The thing is, Bina is rapidly losing any desire to be a conventional 'good girl'. With all that is happening around her, she simply cannot bring herself to join the mainstream of a routine, predictable life. Once she finishes school, she gains admission to Bethune College, where two of her classmates, Suhasini Dutta and Shanti Dasgupta, are involved with a small revolutionary group. As she grows closer to her new friends and is inducted into their group, she is ecstatic at the possibility of using whatever limited skills she possesses in the service of the nation.

In the first half of the 1930s, Bengal is in turmoil, and the British administration is endlessly plagued by Indian revolutionary activities. On 18 April 1930, the outrageous attempt to loot the Chittagong Armoury, led by 'Master Da' Surya Sen, has sent the nation into a frenzy. A few months later, on 25 August, a failed attempt at Dalhousie Square on the life of the all-powerful Commissioner of Police, Charles Tegart, leads to the death of Anuja Charan Sengupta and the arrest of Dinesh Majumdar.

Having shot dead Inspector General Lowman in Dhaka, Benoy Basu becomes a fugitive. But he reappears a while later, alongside Dinesh Gupta and Badal Gupta. On December1930, the trio spark the legendary 'Battle of the Corridors' inside Writers' Building, having assassinated the tyrannical police officer Simpson. As 1931 draws to a close, school girls Shanti Ghosh and Suniti Choudhury pull off the unthinkable, killing Magistrate Stevens of Comilla, for which they are sentenced to deportation for life.

These and many more such blows goad the British government into a state of savage vengeance. Even members of Bina's small group are not spared as arrests become desperate and random. Disturbed and agitated, Bina decides the time has come for her to do something, anything, completely on her own if need be, which will strike at the administration's very foundation, and induce terror among the police.

What can she do, though? The thought keeps her awake all night.

Finally, an idea comes to her like lightning. And she scrambles out of bed. She absolutely must visit Didi today.

'Do you even know what you're saying? You think it's that simple?'

Kamala Dasgupta's first reaction to Bina's master plan is one of incredulous laughter. Born in Dhaka in 1907, Kamala was initiated into the revolutionary ideal as an undergraduate student of Bethune College, and joined the group Jugantar during her postgraduate years. It was in the service of Jugantar that she lived away from her home, as a manager at a women's hostel. An expert in the use of firearms, she acted as arms supplier and arsenal caretaker from the hostel itself.

Bina, of course, is Kamala's classmate Kalyani's younger sister, and also a student at Bethune. Kamala is immensely fond of the cheerful young girl, who is so fixed in her purpose of serving the nation, but she's a little too emotional. Can such a momentous decision as the one she is talking about now be taken solely on the basis of emotions?

'Battles can't be fought on emotions alone, Bina. Besides, it would be a terrible risk. You will be caught, no question, and probably spend the rest of your life in prison. You simply won't be able to continue the fight any longer.'

'Who says I'm basing all this only on emotions, Didi? I'm using my brains too. I know I will be caught, but I'm not going there to escape. And I'm ready for any kind of punishment. Please, stop saying no, and just find me a revolver.'

'What if you're hanged?'

'I'll laugh my way through it, you watch.'

'What about deportation? Can you bear it?'

'Nothing to worry about at all. Shanti and Suniti are there, I'll have a great time teaching them.'

'What if you can't take police torture?'

'I'll try not to give them that chance. I will have potassium cyanide in my pocket.'

Kamala realizes the futility of further objections. The girl's mind is irrevocably made up. Nevertheless, over the next few days, she continues her valiant attempts to talk Bina out of her course of action. Bina remains firm in her decision. Having discussed the matter with her close associate Sudhir Ghosh, Kamala puts together the Rs 280 needed for a revolver, which Sudhir procures. The weapon is a five-chamber .380 bore Belgian revolver, which Kamala hands over to Bina, along with cartridges and the packet of potassium cyanide. And then she explains the mechanism of the firearm.

'This is the barrel, through which the bullet will travel once you press the trigger...the critical thing about shooting is the grip, though...how you hold the weapon...'

6 February 1932. The packed Senate Hall of Calcutta University reverberates with an animated humming.

'We are gathered here today for the annual convocation ceremony of our university. It is a proud day for the students present here, as it is a proud moment for us because adorning the chair of the chief guest for today's programme is His Excellency the Governor of Bengal Sir Stanley Jackson, to whom we are truly grateful for graciously agreeing to spare some of his invaluable time for us...'

Sitting in the fourth row, Bina doesn't take in a single word. Looking around the hall, she notices everyone listening to the vice chancellor's welcome address with great attention. The sight irritates her. What are these people listening to? Year after year, these same words have been repeated. When is he going to finish dishing out the same old hogwash? When will the governor's address begin?

She runs her hand over the revolver tucked into the inside right pocket of her black gown, and then gently touches the potassium cyanide in her left pocket. Finally, she goes over her plan one last time.

Jackson can only be killed once he is out of his seat and has begun to speak. Right now, he's at the absolute centre of the stage, eight more chairs, bearing other distinguished guests, flanking him. It is impossible to attempt anything now. When will his speech begin? She can't stop fidgeting; the sooner the better.

'...And now, our Chief Guest Sir Stanley Jackson will deliver his address, his priceless advice will help guide our students along their future paths...'

Bina's nerves go on instant alert. Finally! The moment has come to strike openly at the domination of the British Raj. Running her hand over the revolver one last time, she thinks back to what Kamala Di has taught her. What was it she had said? Grip is crucial…foresight U…what else? Why can't she remember clearly? She has lost count of the number of dry practice sessions she has gone through over the past week. So why is everything such a blur at the last minute? Her throat is running dry too; some water would have helped. Why is this happening? Is she afraid?

As has been her habit throughout her life whenever she is agitated and needs to calm down, she thinks of her father. Beni Madhab often says, 'Never be afraid of the storms that life casts your way. It's difficult to conquer fear, but not impossible. If you have the courage of your conviction, fear will fear you. When you face fear, stand straight and tall.'

Will he be happy to hear that his beloved daughter has killed the governor? Not really, she thinks. Sitting in their Ekdalia Road home, he will, in fact, be heartbroken. So will Ma. Beni Madhab has always been a thorough patriot, but never a believer in armed revolution. What option does she have, though, given the current situation? How long can a movement remain non-violent in the face of such extreme repression? For how much longer can one offer the other cheek after being slapped on one? Bina rises from her chair.

'Ladies and gentlemen, distinguished guests and my dear students… It is indeed a privilege for me…'

The governor stops midway through the sentence. Why is that girl in a black gown out of her chair and rushing at him? What is she taking out of her pocket? Is that a revolver?!

Tall and well-built, Jackson was extremely physically fit too. A former international cricketer, he played twenty Test matches for England as a batsman and part-time bowler, with a total of 1,415 runs at an average of 48.79, with five centuries. He also took 24 wickets, at an average of 33.29.

As the first bullet explodes out of the chamber, Jackson ducks instantly, as though avoiding a bouncer. The bullet whizzes past, two inches from his head. Amidst the uproar in the Senate Hall, Vice Chancellor Hassan Suhrawardy rushes down from the dais and grabs Bina by the scruff of her neck. Disconcerted by the failed first shot, Bina is disoriented, but still presses the trigger three more times. By now, Jackson has moved to one side, and all three shots miss. Getting over the suddenness of the attack, the plainclothesmen present in the hall finally capture the twenty-one-year-old before she can touch the potassium cyanide.

News of the incident spreads at meteoric speed. A student has shot at the governor at the convocation. He has barely escaped with his life.

The headline in next morning's paper: 'Girl Assassin Shoots at Governor, Misses Target'.

Bina is initially escorted to Elysium Row, and from there to Lalbazar. She doesn't undergo any physical torture during the interrogation, but faces hours of humiliation caused by intensely insulting questions. Despite the best efforts of the police, however, she remains stonily silent. Nevertheless, purely on the basis of suspicion, the police arrest Kamala Dasgupta on 1 March, and she is subsequently sentenced to six years in prison.

The case against Bina is based on Section 307 (attempt to murder) of the Indian Penal Code and the Arms Act, and, because she freely admits to her guilt, the trial is wrapped up in a mere seven days. On 15 February, she is sentenced to nine years of rigorous imprisonment.

Standing in the dock, Bina proudly declares, 'Yes, I wanted to kill the Governor. Unfortunately, I failed. I bear no personal grudge against Stanley Jackson or his family, he is like a father figure, but he is the living image and the supreme symbol of a government, and an administrative system, which has enslaved my country and kept it in chains. I wanted to attack that symbol.'

Jackson may have survived, but Bina's effort did not go to waste. That her fearless mission shook the British government to its very base is evident from contemporary official documents and reports. The administration realized the extent to which a population had to be pushed, and the level of rage, disgust and resentment it had to feel, before a college student could think of mounting a solo attack on the governor. Overnight, security was heightened for senior government officials, who began to fear for their lives, however temporarily.

Two years before term, Bina was pardoned by the Crown, and released in 1939. She then joined the Indian National Congress and played an active role in the Quit India movement, which led to her being arrested yet again, and a three-year prison term. Subsequently, she became a member of the Bengal Provincial Legislative Assembly (West Bengal Legislative Assembly after Independence) from 1946 to 1951. As Independence drew near, she published her memoirs titled *Shringkhal-Jhankar* (The Rattling of Chains), and married fellow revolutionary Jatish Bhaumik in the year of India's Independence.

Her last years were spent in Rishikesh, in the lap of the Himalayas, where she passed away in solitude on 26 October 1986, hidden from the public eye and largely neglected.

There are a few books and other research material on the role played by women during the fiery days of the freedom struggle, but it may be stated without hesitation that the sacrifices made by innumerable devoted patriots like Bina Das have been historically deprived of the publicity and appraisal they deserve.

The time has come to rectify the lapse, to reassess the contributions that Bengal's women made to the freedom movement. The time has also come to recall these words of Kazi Nazrul Islam:

The great creations of our world, blessings incarnate
One half came from the woman, the other from her mate.

Bina Das

Kalyani Das

Kamala Dasgupta

Beni Madhab Das

Stanley Jackson

Senate Hall of Calcutta University